About the Author

Having lived for more than four decades on the only known planet with life, I have been fortunate to witness rapid technological advancements and unfortunate to experience challenges like climate change and terrorism. My job has allowed me to travel extensively, interact with diverse people, and understand various lifestyles, challenges, and best practices.

The writing style in this book will be straightforward, much like the daily communication of billions of people worldwide, avoiding heavy vocabulary that requires a dictionary. This book provides a comprehensive structure for AI, covering foundational concepts, applications, ethical considerations, and future directions. Each chapter will be expanded with detailed explanations and practical examples to create a thorough and engaging read.

I strongly believe that even the most complex problems have simple solutions, though we often complicate them ourselves. Enjoy the read, and feel free to share your feedback or discuss any aspect through email at thinklayman@gmail.com.

Prakash Singh

Table of Content

- Recurrent Neural Networks (RNNs)
- Generative Adversarial Networks (GANs)
- Transformers

12. Training Deep Learning Models

- Data preprocessing and augmentation
- Loss functions and optimization
- Addressing challenges: overfitting, vanishing gradients

Part IV: AI Applications

13. Computer Vision

- Object detection and recognition
- Image segmentation

14. Natural Language Processing (NLP)

- Text processing and analysis
- Language models and transformers (e.g., BERT, GPT)
- Real-world applications: Chatbots, translation, sentiment analysis

15. Robotics and Autonomous Systems

- Basics of robotics
- Integration of AI in robotics
- Applications: Industrial robots, drones, autonomous vehicles

16. AI in Healthcare

- Diagnostic systems
- Personalized medicine
- Challenges and future directions

17. AI in Business and Finance

- Predictive analytics

- The quest for Artificial General Intelligence (AGI)

24. Glossary of AI Terms

Preface

The Importance of Artificial Intelligence in Today's World

Artificial Intelligence (AI) has rapidly become an integral part of modern life, transforming industries, enhancing human capabilities, and addressing complex challenges across the globe. Its significance is underscored by its widespread applications and profound impacts on various sectors, including healthcare, business, finance, education, and environmental sustainability.

Healthcare Transformation

AI is revolutionizing healthcare by improving diagnostics, treatment planning, and patient care. Machine learning algorithms can analyze medical images with high precision, facilitating early detection of diseases such as cancer. AI-driven predictive analytics allow for personalized treatment plans tailored to individual patients' genetic profiles and medical histories. Moreover, AI-powered monitoring systems track patient vitals and alert healthcare providers to potential issues, enabling timely interventions and improving patient outcomes. This technological advancement not only augments the capabilities of healthcare professionals but also makes healthcare more efficient and accessible.

Business Efficiency and Innovation

In the business world, AI is a key driver of efficiency and innovation. Companies utilize AI for customer service, supply chain management, and data-driven decision-making. Natural language processing (NLP) enables the development of chatbots and virtual assistants that provide 24/7 customer support, enhancing customer satisfaction and operational efficiency. Predictive analytics help businesses anticipate market trends, optimize inventory levels, and make informed decisions. Additionally, AI-powered automation streamlines repetitive tasks, freeing up human resources for strategic and creative activities. This boost in productivity fosters innovation and allows businesses to stay competitive in a rapidly evolving market.

Financial Sector Advancements

The financial industry heavily relies on AI to enhance security, optimize operations, and provide personalized services. AI algorithms detect fraudulent transactions, assess credit risks, and develop sophisticated investment strategies. By analyzing vast amounts of data in real-time, AI systems identify suspicious activities and anomalies that might elude human analysts, thus safeguarding financial transactions. AI-driven robo-advisors offer personalized investment advice, democratizing financial planning and making it accessible to a broader audience. These advancements contribute to a more secure and efficient financial ecosystem.

Educational Enhancements

AI is also transforming education by personalizing learning experiences and supporting educators. Adaptive learning platforms use AI to tailor educational content to the individual needs and learning styles of students, enhancing engagement and improving outcomes. AI-powered tools assist teachers by automating administrative tasks, grading assignments, and providing insights into student performance. This allows educators to focus more on teaching and mentoring, ultimately enriching the educational experience. The integration of AI in education ensures that learning is more accessible, personalized, and effective.

Environmental Sustainability

AI plays a critical role in promoting environmental sustainability. Predictive models powered by AI forecast weather patterns, track environmental changes, and manage natural resources more efficiently. AI algorithms optimize energy consumption in smart grids, reducing waste and promoting renewable energy sources. In agriculture, AI-driven technologies enable precision farming, which maximizes crop yields while minimizing the use of water, fertilizers, and pesticides. By providing actionable insights, AI helps create sustainable practices that mitigate the impact of human activities on the environment.

Human Capability Enhancement and Innovation

AI enhances human capabilities by automating mundane tasks, allowing individuals to focus on more creative and strategic endeavors. This shift not only boosts productivity but also drives innovation by encouraging the exploration of new ideas and solutions. In research and development, AI accelerates scientific discoveries by analyzing large datasets, identifying patterns, and generating hypotheses at an unprecedented pace. This collaborative synergy between humans and AI leads to groundbreaking advancements and opens up new possibilities across various fields.

The Evolution of Artificial Intelligence

The journey of Artificial Intelligence (AI) has been marked by remarkable advancements and milestones that have progressively transformed it from a theoretical concept to a central technology in modern society. The evolution of AI can be traced through several distinct phases, each characterized by significant breakthroughs and shifts in understanding.

Early Beginnings and Foundations

The concept of intelligent machines dates back to ancient mythology, but the formal foundation of AI began in the mid-20th century. In 1950, British mathematician and logician Alan Turing proposed the idea of a machine that could mimic human intelligence in his seminal paper "Computing Machinery and Intelligence." Turing introduced the Turing Test as a criterion to determine whether a machine could exhibit intelligent behavior indistinguishable from that of a human.

In 1956, the Dartmouth Conference, organized by John McCarthy, Marvin Minsky, Nathaniel Rochester, and Claude Shannon, is widely regarded as the birth of AI as a field of study. This event brought together leading researchers to discuss the potential of creating machines that could think and learn, coining the term "Artificial Intelligence."

The Golden Age of AI (1950s-1970s)

The period following the Dartmouth Conference saw rapid developments in AI research. Early AI programs, such as the Logic Theorist (developed by Allen Newell and Herbert A. Simon) and the General Problem Solver, demonstrated that machines could perform tasks that required human-like reasoning and problem-solving abilities. Researchers developed symbolic AI, which relied on explicitly programmed rules and logic to mimic human decision-making processes.

In the 1960s and 1970s, AI research received substantial funding and interest, leading to the development of expert systems—computer programs that emulated the decision-making abilities of human experts in specific domains. Notable examples include DENDRAL, a system for chemical analysis, and MYCIN, a medical diagnosis system.

The AI Winter and Renewed Interest (1980s-1990s)

Despite early successes, AI faced significant challenges, leading to periods of reduced funding and interest, known as "AI winters." The limitations of symbolic AI and expert systems became apparent as they struggled with scalability and real-world complexity. The optimism of the early days waned, and AI research slowed.

However, the 1980s and 1990s saw renewed interest in AI, driven by advances in computing power and the emergence of machine learning—a subfield of AI focused on algorithms that allow computers to learn from data. Neural networks, inspired by the human brain's structure, gained attention for their potential to model complex patterns and relationships in data.

The Rise of Machine Learning and Big Data (2000s-Present)

The turn of the millennium marked a significant shift in AI research, with the advent of machine learning and big data analytics. Machine learning algorithms, such as support vector machines, decision trees, and ensemble methods, became more sophisticated and widely adopted. The availability of vast amounts of data and increased computational power facilitated the training of complex models.

Deep learning, a subfield of machine learning, revolutionized AI with the development of deep neural networks. In 2012, a breakthrough came with AlexNet, a deep convolutional neural network that dramatically improved image recognition performance. This success spurred a wave of innovations in various domains, including natural language processing, speech recognition, and autonomous systems.

Modern AI and Future Directions

Today, AI is ubiquitous, powering technologies that impact daily life, from virtual assistants and recommendation systems to autonomous vehicles and medical diagnostics. Advances in natural language processing, exemplified by models like BERT and GPT-3, have enabled machines to understand and generate human language with remarkable accuracy.

The future of AI holds promise for even more profound advancements. Research is focused on achieving Artificial General Intelligence (AGI), machines with the ability to understand, learn, and apply knowledge across a wide range of tasks at a human-like level. Ethical considerations, transparency, and accountability are also becoming increasingly important as AI systems are integrated into critical societal functions.

Purpose and Scope of the Book

Purpose

The primary purpose of this book is to provide a comprehensive and accessible understanding of Artificial Intelligence (AI) to a broad audience, including students, professionals, enthusiasts, and policymakers. In a world where AI is increasingly becoming a central technology across various sectors, it is crucial to demystify its concepts, applications, and implications. This book aims to bridge the knowledge gap by offering clear explanations, practical insights, and real-world examples of how AI is shaping our present and future.

The book seeks to achieve the following objectives:

1. Educate: To educate readers about the fundamental concepts of AI, including its history, underlying technologies, and key methodologies. By building a solid foundation, readers will gain a deep understanding of how AI works and its potential.

2. Inform: To inform readers about the diverse applications of AI across different industries such as healthcare, finance, education, and environmental sustainability. This includes showcasing success stories, current trends, and the transformative impact of AI on various domains.

3. Engage: To engage readers with thought-provoking discussions on the ethical, legal, and social implications of AI. This book will address concerns such as bias, privacy, job displacement, and the future of human-AI collaboration, encouraging readers to think critically about these issues.

4. Empower: To empower readers with the knowledge to leverage AI in their respective fields. Whether it's through understanding basic machine learning techniques, deploying AI solutions, or making informed decisions about AI adoption, this book aims to provide practical guidance.

Scope

The scope of the book encompasses a wide range of topics, structured to cover both the breadth and depth of AI. The content is organized to gradually build the reader's knowledge from fundamental concepts to advanced applications and future prospects.

1. Foundations of AI

   - History and Evolution: Tracing the origins and milestones in AI development.

   - Basic Concepts: Understanding AI, machine learning, and deep learning.

   - Key Technologies: Introduction to algorithms, neural networks, and data processing.

2. Core Areas of AI

   - Machine Learning: Supervised, unsupervised, and reinforcement learning.

   - Deep Learning: Neural networks, CNNs, RNNs, and advanced architectures.

   - Natural Language Processing: Text analysis, language models, and applications.

3. AI Applications

   - Healthcare: Diagnostics, treatment planning, and patient monitoring.

   - Business: Customer service, predictive analytics, and automation.

   - Finance: Fraud detection, credit scoring, and investment strategies.

   - Education: Personalized learning, AI in teaching, and educational tools.

   - Environmental Sustainability: Climate modeling, resource management, and precision agriculture.

4. Ethical, Legal, and Social Implications

- Ethical Considerations: Bias, fairness, transparency, and accountability.

- Legal Frameworks: Current regulations, future challenges, and case studies.

- Social Impact: Employment, human-AI collaboration, and societal change.

5. Future of AI

- Emerging Trends: Innovations, quantum computing, and AI in new domains.

- Human-AI Synergy: Enhancing human capabilities, collaborative intelligence.

- Speculative Futures: Artificial General Intelligence (AGI) and beyond.

6. Practical Guidance

- Implementing AI: Tools, frameworks, and best practices for AI deployment.

- Case Studies: Real-world examples of successful AI implementations.

- Resources: Further reading, educational resources, and AI communities.

What is Artificial Intelligence?

Definition and Scope of Artificial Intelligence (AI)

Definition

Artificial Intelligence (AI) refers to the simulation of human intelligence in machines that are programmed to think, learn, and perform tasks typically requiring human intelligence. AI encompasses a broad range of techniques, methodologies, and applications aimed at enabling computers to mimic human cognitive functions such as reasoning, problem-solving, perception, learning, and language understanding. The ultimate goal of AI is to develop machines that exhibit intelligence, adaptability, and autonomy, allowing them to perform tasks autonomously and interact with their environment in a manner that resembles human intelligence.

Scope

The scope of Artificial Intelligence is vast and encompasses various domains, technologies, and applications. It includes but is not limited to the following areas:

1. Machine Learning: Machine learning is a subset of AI that focuses on developing algorithms and models that allow computers to learn from data and make predictions or decisions without explicit programming. This includes supervised learning, unsupervised learning, reinforcement learning, and deep learning techniques.

2. Deep Learning: Deep learning is a specialized area of machine learning that utilizes artificial neural networks with multiple layers to model complex patterns and relationships in data. It has been particularly successful in tasks such as image recognition, natural language processing, and speech recognition.

3. Natural Language Processing (NLP): NLP is a branch of AI that focuses on enabling computers to understand, interpret, and generate human language. It involves tasks such as speech recognition, language translation, sentiment analysis, and text summarization.

4. Computer Vision: Computer vision is the field of AI that deals with enabling computers to interpret and analyze visual information from the real world. It

includes tasks such as object detection, image classification, facial recognition, and scene understanding.

5. Robotics and Autonomous Systems: Robotics involves the design, development, and deployment of autonomous systems that can perceive their environment, make decisions, and perform physical tasks. AI plays a crucial role in enabling robots to navigate, manipulate objects, and interact with humans safely and intelligently.

6. Expert Systems: Expert systems are AI applications that emulate the decision-making abilities of human experts in specific domains. They use knowledge representation, inference engines, and rule-based reasoning to provide expert-level advice, diagnosis, or problem-solving capabilities.

7. Data Mining and Predictive Analytics: AI techniques are used in data mining and predictive analytics to discover patterns, trends, and insights from large datasets. This includes techniques such as clustering, classification, regression, and anomaly detection, which are used in various industries for decision support and forecasting.

8. Autonomous Vehicles: AI is driving the development of autonomous vehicles, including self-driving cars, drones, and unmanned aerial vehicles (UAVs). These vehicles use AI algorithms for perception, decision-making, and control to navigate safely and efficiently in complex environments.

9. Virtual Assistants and Chatbots: Virtual assistants and chatbots are AI-powered applications that interact with users in natural language to provide information, answer questions, and perform tasks. They use NLP, machine learning, and dialog management techniques to understand user intent and generate appropriate responses.

10. Ethical, Legal, and Social Implications: The ethical, legal, and social implications of AI are an integral part of its scope. This includes considerations such as bias and fairness, transparency and accountability, privacy and security, job displacement, and the impact on society at large.

The Distinction between AI, Machine Learning, and Deep Learning

Artificial Intelligence (AI)

Definition: Artificial Intelligence (AI) is a broad field of computer science focused on creating systems that can perform tasks that typically require human intelligence. These tasks include reasoning, problem-solving, learning, perception, and language understanding.

Scope: AI encompasses a wide range of techniques, methodologies, and applications aimed at enabling machines to mimic human cognitive functions. This includes symbolic AI, expert systems, natural language processing, computer vision, robotics, and autonomous systems.

Characteristics:

- AI systems can perform a wide variety of tasks, ranging from simple to complex.

- They can adapt to changing environments and learn from experience.

- AI systems may incorporate a combination of rule-based logic, statistical methods, and machine learning algorithms.

Machine Learning

Definition: Machine Learning (ML) is a subset of AI that focuses on developing algorithms and models that enable computers to learn from data and make predictions or decisions without being explicitly programmed.

Scope: Machine learning algorithms learn patterns and relationships from labeled or unlabeled data, allowing computers to generalize and make predictions on new, unseen data. ML techniques include supervised learning, unsupervised learning, reinforcement learning, and semi-supervised learning.

Characteristics:

- Machine learning algorithms improve their performance over time through experience and exposure to data.

- They can handle large and complex datasets, making them suitable for tasks such as pattern recognition, classification, regression, and clustering.

- ML models require labeled training data to learn from, and their performance is evaluated based on metrics such as accuracy, precision, recall, and F1 score.

Deep Learning

Definition: Deep Learning (DL) is a subfield of machine learning that focuses on developing artificial neural networks with multiple layers (deep architectures) to model complex patterns and relationships in data.

Scope: Deep learning techniques, inspired by the structure and function of the human brain, have achieved remarkable success in tasks such as image recognition, speech recognition, natural language processing, and reinforcement learning.

Characteristics:

- Deep learning models consist of interconnected layers of neurons, including input, hidden, and output layers.

- They automatically learn hierarchical representations of data through the process of feature learning, without the need for manual feature engineering.

- DL models require large amounts of labeled data and computational resources for training, but they can achieve state-of-the-art performance on a wide range of tasks.

Comparison

- Scope: AI is the broadest term, encompassing all efforts to create systems that can mimic human intelligence. Machine learning is a subset of AI that focuses on developing algorithms that allow computers to learn from data. Deep learning is a subset of machine learning that focuses on developing artificial neural networks with multiple layers.

- Approach: AI encompasses various approaches, including symbolic reasoning, expert systems, and statistical methods. Machine learning focuses on developing algorithms that enable computers to learn from data. Deep learning relies on artificial neural networks with multiple layers to model complex patterns and relationships in data.

- Applications: AI has diverse applications, including natural language processing, computer vision, robotics, and expert systems. Machine learning is used for tasks such as classification, regression, clustering, and reinforcement learning. Deep learning has achieved success in tasks such as image recognition, speech recognition, and natural language processing.

Historical Context and Evolution of Artificial Intelligence (AI)

Early Beginnings

The roots of Artificial Intelligence (AI) can be traced back to ancient myths and legends that depicted intelligent machines and automata. However, the formal foundation of AI as a field of study began in the mid-20th century.

1950s: Birth of AI

In 1950, British mathematician and logician Alan Turing proposed the "Turing Test" as a criterion for determining whether a machine exhibits intelligent behavior indistinguishable from that of a human. This concept laid the groundwork for AI research and sparked interest in creating machines capable of human-like cognition.

1956: The Dartmouth Conference

The seminal event that is widely regarded as the birth of AI as a field of study was the Dartmouth Conference in 1956. Organized by John McCarthy, Marvin Minsky, Nathaniel Rochester, and Claude Shannon, the conference brought together leading researchers from various disciplines to discuss the possibility of creating machines that could think and learn. This event marked the formal inception of AI as an interdisciplinary field.

1950s-1960s: Early Developments

During the late 1950s and 1960s, significant progress was made in developing AI systems capable of reasoning and problem-solving. Early AI programs, such as the Logic Theorist developed by Allen Newell and Herbert A. Simon, demonstrated that machines could perform tasks that required human-like reasoning and intelligence. This era saw the emergence of symbolic AI, which relied on explicitly programmed rules and logic to mimic human decision-making processes.

1970s: AI Winter

Despite early successes, the field of AI faced significant challenges and setbacks in the 1970s. The limitations of symbolic AI and expert systems became apparent as they struggled to handle real-world complexity and scalability. Funding for AI research declined, leading to what is known as the "AI Winter," a period of reduced interest and investment in AI.

1980s-1990s: Renewed Interest

The 1980s and 1990s saw a resurgence of interest in AI, fueled by advances in computing power, algorithms, and methodologies. Machine learning, a subset of AI focused on developing algorithms that enable computers to learn from data, gained prominence during this period. Researchers explored new approaches such as neural networks, genetic algorithms, and fuzzy logic, leading to significant progress in AI research.

21st Century: Rise of Machine Learning and Deep Learning

The turn of the millennium marked a new era of AI driven by advances in machine learning and data-driven approaches. Machine learning algorithms became more sophisticated and widely adopted, fueled by the availability of large datasets and increased computational power. Deep learning, a subfield of machine learning focused on developing artificial neural networks with multiple layers, emerged as a powerful technique for modeling complex patterns and relationships in data. Breakthroughs in deep learning led to significant advancements in tasks such as image recognition, speech recognition, and natural language processing.

Present and Future

Today, AI is ubiquitous, powering technologies that impact virtually every aspect of modern life. From virtual assistants and recommendation systems to autonomous vehicles and medical diagnostics, AI is transforming industries and reshaping society. As AI continues to evolve, researchers are exploring new frontiers such as Artificial General Intelligence (AGI), which aims to create machines with human-like cognitive abilities. Ethical, legal, and societal implications of AI are also receiving increasing attention, highlighting the need for responsible and ethical AI development and deployment.

Part I: Foundations of AI

The History of AI

Early Developments and Pioneers of Artificial Intelligence (AI)

The history of Artificial Intelligence (AI) is filled with groundbreaking discoveries, innovative ideas, and visionary pioneers who laid the foundation for the field as we know it today. Here are some of the early developments and key figures in the evolution of AI:

Alan Turing

Alan Turing, a British mathematician, logician, and computer scientist, is often considered the father of theoretical computer science and artificial intelligence. In his seminal paper "Computing Machinery and Intelligence" published in 1950, Turing introduced the concept of the Turing Test, proposing a criterion for determining whether a machine exhibits intelligent behavior indistinguishable from that of a human. His work laid the theoretical groundwork for AI and sparked interest in the possibility of creating intelligent machines.

John McCarthy

John McCarthy, an American computer scientist, coined the term "Artificial Intelligence" and organized the Dartmouth Conference in 1956, which is widely regarded as the birth of AI as a field of study. McCarthy's vision was to create machines that could think and learn, leading to the development of symbolic AI and the exploration of topics such as problem-solving, natural language understanding, and machine learning.

Herbert A. Simon and Allen Newell

Herbert A. Simon and Allen Newell, both pioneers in the field of cognitive psychology and computer science, collaborated on the development of the Logic Theorist in the late 1950s. The Logic Theorist was one of the earliest AI programs capable of solving mathematical problems using symbolic reasoning and heuristic search. Simon and Newell's work laid the foundation for the development of symbolic AI and demonstrated that machines could perform tasks requiring human-like reasoning and intelligence.

Marvin Minsky

Marvin Minsky, an American cognitive scientist and computer scientist, made significant contributions to the early development of AI. Along with John McCarthy, Minsky co-founded the MIT AI Laboratory in 1959, where he conducted pioneering research in areas such as neural networks, robotics, and machine perception. Minsky's influential book "Perceptrons," co-authored with Seymour Papert in 1969, explored the limitations of early neural network models and laid the groundwork for future developments in deep learning.

Arthur Samuel

Arthur Samuel, an American computer scientist and pioneer in machine learning, is best known for developing the first self-learning program, known as the Samuel Checkers-playing Program, in the late 1950s. Using a technique called "adaptive learning," Samuel's program improved its performance over time through experience and exposure to data, paving the way for future developments in machine learning and reinforcement learning.

Key Milestones in AI Research

Artificial Intelligence (AI) research has witnessed numerous significant milestones over the years, marking breakthroughs in understanding, innovation, and technological advancement. Here are some key milestones that have shaped the field of AI:

1950s: Birth of AI

- 1950: Alan Turing proposes the Turing Test as a criterion for determining whether a machine exhibits intelligent behavior indistinguishable from that of a human.

- 1956: The Dartmouth Conference, organized by John McCarthy, Marvin Minsky, Nathaniel Rochester, and Claude Shannon, marks the formal inception of AI as a field of study. The conference establishes AI's goals and methods and sets the stage for future research.

1960s: Early Developments

- 1963: John McCarthy and his team develop the LISP programming language, which becomes the primary language for AI research and development.

- 1966: The development of the ELIZA program by Joseph Weizenbaum demonstrates the potential for natural language processing and human-computer interaction.

1970s: AI Winter

- 1970s: The limitations of symbolic AI and expert systems become apparent, leading to a period of reduced interest and funding known as the "AI Winter."

1980s-1990s: Renewed Interest

- 1980s: Expert systems gain popularity as AI researchers explore rule-based approaches to mimic human decision-making.

- 1985: Backpropagation, a method for training artificial neural networks, is rediscovered and contributes to advancements in neural network research.

- 1997: IBM's Deep Blue defeats chess world champion Garry Kasparov, demonstrating the potential of AI in strategic decision-making.

2000s: Rise of Machine Learning

- 2006: Geoffrey Hinton, Yoshua Bengio, and Yann LeCun pioneer the use of deep learning techniques in machine learning, leading to breakthroughs in speech recognition and computer vision.

- 2011: IBM's Watson defeats human champions in the quiz show Jeopardy!, showcasing advancements in natural language processing and question-answering systems.

2010s: Deep Learning Dominance

- 2012: AlexNet, a deep convolutional neural network developed by Alex Krizhevsky, Ilya Sutskever, and Geoffrey Hinton, wins the ImageNet competition, significantly improving image recognition accuracy.

- 2014: Google's DeepMind develops AlphaGo, an AI program that defeats world champion Go player Lee Sedol, demonstrating the power of deep reinforcement learning.

- 2019: OpenAI's GPT-2 model achieves state-of-the-art performance in natural language processing tasks, including text generation and language understanding.

Present and Future

- 2020s: AI continues to advance rapidly, with developments in areas such as reinforcement learning, autonomous systems, and ethical AI. Research focuses on achieving Artificial General Intelligence (AGI) and addressing societal challenges associated with AI deployment.

The Rise of Machine Learning and Deep Learning

Machine Learning (ML) and Deep Learning (DL) have emerged as transformative technologies that have revolutionized various industries and reshaped the landscape of artificial intelligence. The rise of ML and DL has been driven by a combination of factors, including advancements in algorithms, increased computational power, and the availability of large datasets. Here's a detailed look at how machine learning and deep learning have evolved and gained prominence:

Early Developments in Machine Learning

The roots of machine learning can be traced back to the mid-20th century, with pioneers such as Arthur Samuel and Frank Rosenblatt making significant contributions. Arthur Samuel's work on the development of the first self-learning program for playing checkers in the late 1950s laid the foundation for the concept of machine learning. Frank Rosenblatt's invention of the perceptron, a type of artificial neural network, in 1957 introduced the idea of using computational models inspired by the human brain for learning and pattern recognition tasks.

Evolution of Machine Learning Algorithms

In the following decades, researchers developed a wide range of machine learning algorithms and techniques, including decision trees, nearest neighbor algorithms, support vector machines, and Bayesian networks. These algorithms enabled computers to learn from data, make predictions, and perform tasks without being explicitly programmed.

Rise of Deep Learning

Deep learning, a subfield of machine learning, gained prominence in the 2000s with the pioneering work of Geoffrey Hinton, Yoshua Bengio, and Yann LeCun. Deep learning techniques, inspired by the structure and function of the human brain, involve training artificial neural networks with multiple layers (deep architectures) to model complex patterns and relationships in data.

Breakthroughs in Deep Learning

The breakthroughs in deep learning were catalyzed by the availability of large datasets, increased computational power, and advances in algorithmic techniques such as backpropagation and convolutional neural networks (CNNs). In 2012, AlexNet, a deep CNN developed by Alex Krizhevsky, Ilya Sutskever, and Geoffrey Hinton, won the ImageNet competition, significantly improving image recognition accuracy and demonstrating the potential of deep learning.

Applications of Machine Learning and Deep Learning

Machine learning and deep learning have found applications across various domains, including computer vision, natural language processing, speech recognition, healthcare, finance, and autonomous systems. Deep learning models have achieved state-of-the-art performance in tasks such as image recognition, object detection, language translation, and game playing.

Future Directions

As machine learning and deep learning continue to evolve, researchers are exploring new frontiers and addressing challenges such as interpretability, scalability, and robustness. Future directions in ML and DL include advancements in reinforcement learning, generative modeling, federated learning, and ethical AI. These technologies hold the promise of driving further innovation and creating new opportunities for solving complex problems in diverse fields.

Basic Concepts in AI

Agents and Environments in Artificial Intelligence

In the field of Artificial Intelligence (AI), agents and environments play a fundamental role in modeling and understanding intelligent behavior. An agent is an entity that perceives its environment through sensors and acts upon it through effectors to achieve specific goals. The environment, on the other hand, is the external system or context in which the agent operates. Here's a detailed exploration of agents and environments in AI:

Agents

An agent is an autonomous entity that perceives its environment and acts upon it to achieve its goals. Agents can range from simple systems, such as reactive machines, to complex systems, such as intelligent robots or software agents. The design and behavior of an agent depend on its perception, knowledge, decision-making capabilities, and interaction with the environment. Agents can be classified based on various criteria, including:

- Autonomy: Agents may operate autonomously or collaboratively with other agents.

- Sensing: Agents perceive their environment through sensors, which provide information about the state of the environment.

- Acting: Agents act upon the environment through effectors, which allow them to manipulate their surroundings.

- Learning: Some agents have the ability to learn and adapt their behavior over time through experience.

Environments

The environment is the external system or context in which an agent operates. It encompasses everything that is external to the agent and can influence its behavior. Environments can vary widely in complexity, dynamics, and characteristics, ranging from simple deterministic worlds to complex, uncertain domains. The environment provides the context within which agents perceive, reason, and act to achieve their goals. Environments can be characterized by various factors, including:

- Perceptible Properties: The properties of the environment that are observable or perceivable by the agent through its sensors.

- State Space: The set of all possible states that the environment can be in, which may be discrete or continuous.

- Action Space: The set of all possible actions that the agent can take, which may be deterministic or stochastic.

- Dynamicity: The degree to which the environment changes over time, either in response to the agent's actions or external factors.

- Uncertainty: The presence of uncertainty or randomness in the environment, which may affect the agent's perception and decision-making.

Agent-Environment Interaction

The interaction between agents and environments forms the basis of AI systems. Agents perceive their environment through sensors, which provide information about the current state of the environment. Based on this perception, agents make decisions about how to act to achieve their goals. These actions are then executed through effectors, which can change the state of the environment. The environment responds to the agent's actions by transitioning to a new state, which is perceived by the agent, thus completing the cycle of perception, decision-making, and action.

Examples

- Robotics: A robotic vacuum cleaner is an agent that perceives its environment (the room) through sensors (such as cameras or proximity sensors) and acts upon it by moving and cleaning the floor.

- Autonomous Vehicles: An autonomous car is an agent that perceives its environment (the road and surrounding traffic) through sensors (such as cameras, lidar, and radar) and acts upon it by steering, accelerating, and braking to navigate safely to its destination.

- Software Agents: A software agent deployed on a computer network is an agent that perceives its environment (network traffic, system logs) through sensors (network monitors, log files) and acts upon it by analyzing data, detecting anomalies, and responding to security threats.

AI Problem-Solving Approaches

Problem-solving lies at the heart of Artificial Intelligence (AI), where the goal is to develop algorithms and systems that can effectively find solutions to complex problems. Over the years, AI researchers have devised various problem-solving approaches, each with its own strengths, weaknesses, and suitability for different types of problems. Here's an overview of some common AI problem-solving approaches:

1. Search Algorithms

Search algorithms form the basis of many AI problem-solving techniques, where the goal is to systematically explore a space of possible solutions to find an optimal or satisfactory solution. Some common search algorithms include:

- Depth-First Search (DFS): Explores as far as possible along each branch before backtracking.

- Breadth-First Search (BFS): Explores all neighbor nodes at the present depth before moving on to the nodes at the next depth level.

- A* Search: Uses heuristics to guide the search towards the most promising paths, balancing between the cost of the path and the estimated cost to the goal.

2. Heuristic Search

Heuristic search algorithms incorporate domain-specific knowledge or heuristics to guide the search process more effectively towards the goal state. Examples include:

- Greedy Best-First Search: Expands the node that appears to be closest to the goal based on a heuristic evaluation function.

- Iterative Deepening A* (IDA*): An extension of depth-first search that uses a heuristic to determine the depth limit at each iteration.

3. Constraint Satisfaction Problems (CSP)

In constraint satisfaction problems, the goal is to find a solution that satisfies a set of constraints or conditions. CSPs are commonly used in scheduling, planning, and resource allocation problems. Approaches to solving CSPs include:

- Backtracking: Systematically explores potential solutions, backtracking when a dead-end is encountered.

- Constraint Propagation: Uses inference techniques to reduce the search space by enforcing constraints locally.

4. Evolutionary Algorithms

Evolutionary algorithms are inspired by biological evolution and natural selection, where populations of candidate solutions undergo selection, reproduction, and mutation to evolve towards better solutions. Examples include:

- Genetic Algorithms: Represent candidate solutions as chromosomes and apply genetic operators such as mutation and crossover to generate new solutions.

- Evolution Strategies: Iteratively optimize a population of solutions using randomized mutation and recombination operators.

5. Machine Learning

Machine learning techniques, particularly supervised and reinforcement learning, can be used to learn problem-solving strategies from data or experience. Examples include:

- Supervised Learning: Learns a mapping from input features to output labels based on labeled training data, enabling classification or regression tasks.

- Reinforcement Learning: Learns to make sequential decisions through trial and error, receiving feedback from the environment in the form of rewards or penalties.

6. Logic-Based Approaches

Logic-based approaches represent problems and solutions using formal logic, enabling reasoning and inference. Examples include:

- Predicate Logic: Represents knowledge using logical predicates and performs inference using rules of deduction.

- Expert Systems: Encode domain knowledge as a set of rules or facts and use inference engines to derive conclusions.

Search algorithms and optimization

Search algorithms and optimization play a crucial role in artificial intelligence (AI) by enabling systems to efficiently explore and find solutions to complex problems. Here's a description of search algorithms and optimization techniques:

1. Search Algorithms: Search algorithms are methods used to systematically explore a space of possible solutions to find an optimal or satisfactory solution. These algorithms vary in their strategies for traversing the search space and can be categorized into several types:

   o Uninformed Search Algorithms: These algorithms do not have any additional information about the problem other than the problem definition. Examples include:

     ▪ Breadth-First Search (BFS): Explores all neighbor nodes at the present depth prior to moving on to the nodes at the next depth level.

     ▪ Depth-First Search (DFS): Traverses through the depth of a subtree before backtracking.

     ▪ Uniform Cost Search: Expands the node with the lowest path cost.

   o Informed Search Algorithms (Heuristic Search): These algorithms utilize problem-specific knowledge, known as heuristics, to guide the search towards the most promising areas of the search space. Examples include:

     ▪ A Search*: Evaluates nodes by combining the cost to reach a node with an estimate of the cost to reach the goal from that node.

     ▪ Greedy Best-First Search: Selects the node that is estimated to be closest to the goal.

- ○ Local Search Algorithms: These algorithms focus on improving a single solution iteratively by making small modifications. Examples include:

    - ▪ Hill Climbing: Iteratively moves in the direction of increasing value, terminating when no neighbor has a higher value.

    - ▪ Simulated Annealing: Allows for occasional moves to worse solutions to escape local optima.

2. Optimization Techniques: Optimization in AI refers to the process of improving the performance or efficiency of an AI system. This can involve optimizing parameters, algorithms, or models to achieve better results. Some common optimization techniques include:

    - ○ Gradient Descent: An iterative optimization algorithm used to minimize a loss function by adjusting parameters in the direction of the steepest descent of the gradient.

    - ○ Genetic Algorithms: Inspired by the process of natural selection, genetic algorithms use techniques such as mutation, crossover, and selection to evolve a population of candidate solutions towards an optimal solution.

    - ○ Particle Swarm Optimization: Inspired by the social behavior of organisms such as bird flocking or fish schooling, particle swarm optimization iteratively improves a population of candidate solutions by adjusting their positions in the search space based on their own best known position and the global best known position.

    - ○ Ant Colony Optimization: Inspired by the foraging behavior of ants, this optimization technique iteratively constructs solutions by simulating the movement of virtual ants on a graph representation of the problem domain.

These search algorithms and optimization techniques are fundamental to various applications of AI, including problem-solving, planning, machine learning, and more. By efficiently exploring and optimizing the search space, AI systems can find solutions to complex problems in diverse domains.

Data is the lifeblood of artificial intelligence (AI), serving as the foundation upon which AI systems learn, make decisions, and generate insights. The importance of data in AI can be described across several key aspects:

1. Training AI Models: AI models, whether they are based on machine learning, deep learning, or other techniques, require vast amounts of data to learn patterns, relationships, and features from. The quality, quantity, and diversity of data directly impact the performance and accuracy of these models. Without sufficient and relevant data, AI systems may struggle to generalize well to new, unseen examples and may be prone to biases or inaccuracies.

2. Improving Performance: More data often leads to better AI performance. As AI models are exposed to a larger and more varied dataset, they can learn more robust representations and make more accurate predictions or decisions. Continuous feeding of new data allows AI systems to adapt and improve over time, ensuring that they remain relevant and effective in dynamic environments.

3. Ensuring Fairness and Mitigating Bias: Data quality and diversity are crucial for ensuring fairness and mitigating biases in AI systems. Biases present in training data can propagate into AI models, leading to discriminatory outcomes or unfair decisions. By carefully curating datasets to be representative and inclusive, and by employing techniques such as bias detection and mitigation, AI developers can work towards creating more equitable and unbiased systems.

4. Enabling Personalization and Customization: Personalized and customized experiences in AI applications, such as recommendation systems, virtual assistants, and targeted marketing, rely heavily on data about individual users' preferences, behaviors, and interactions. By analyzing and understanding user data, AI systems can tailor their responses and recommendations to better meet the needs and preferences of individual users, enhancing user satisfaction and engagement.

5. Driving Innovation and Insights: Data fuels innovation and drives the generation of new insights in AI research and development. By analyzing large datasets, AI practitioners can uncover hidden patterns, correlations, and trends that may not be apparent through traditional analysis methods. These insights can lead to breakthroughs in various fields, including healthcare, finance, transportation, and more, enabling advancements and discoveries that benefit society as a whole.

Data and Algorithms

Importance of data in AI

Data can be broadly classified into three main types: structured, unstructured, and semi-structured. These classifications are based on the organization and format of the data, which significantly impacts how it can be stored, processed, and analyzed. Here's a description of each type:

1. Structured Data: Structured data refers to data that is organized into a predefined format with well-defined fields, records, and relationships. This type of data is highly organized and follows a rigid schema, making it easy to store, query, and analyze using traditional database management systems (DBMS). Examples of structured data include:

   o Relational databases: Tables with rows and columns, where each column represents a specific attribute and each row represents a unique record.

   o Spreadsheets: Grids of cells organized into rows and columns, where each cell contains a piece of data.

   o CSV (Comma-Separated Values) files: Text files that store tabular data with each record separated by commas.

Structured data is commonly used in business applications, financial systems, and transactional databases due to its simplicity and ease of processing.

2. Unstructured Data: Unstructured data refers to data that does not have a predefined data model or organizational structure. It lacks a consistent format and can exist in various forms, including text documents, images, audio files, videos, social media posts, emails, and sensor data. Examples of unstructured data include:

   o Text documents: Such as articles, reports, emails, and social media posts.

   o Multimedia files: Including images, audio recordings, and videos.

   o Web pages: HTML documents, blog posts, and online articles.

- Sensor data: Readings from IoT devices, such as temperature, humidity, and GPS coordinates.

Unstructured data is abundant and accounts for a significant portion of the data generated daily. Analyzing unstructured data requires advanced techniques such as natural language processing (NLP), computer vision, and sentiment analysis to extract meaningful insights.

3. Semi-Structured Data: Semi-structured data shares characteristics of both structured and unstructured data. It does not conform to a strict schema like structured data but contains some organizational elements that provide a partial structure. Semi-structured data often includes metadata or tags that provide additional context or hierarchy to the data. Examples of semi-structured data include:

- XML (Extensible Markup Language) files: Text-based files with hierarchical data organized using tags.

- JSON (JavaScript Object Notation) files: Lightweight data interchange format used to represent structured data in a human-readable format.

- NoSQL databases: Databases designed to handle semi-structured and unstructured data, offering flexible schemas and horizontal scalability.

Semi-structured data is prevalent in modern web applications, document storage systems, and data interchange formats due to its flexibility and adaptability to evolving data requirements.

Types of Data: Structured, Unstructured, and Semi-Structured

In the realm of data science and machine learning, data can be broadly categorized into three types: structured, unstructured, and semi-structured. Each type of data has unique characteristics and requires different methods for storage, processing, and analysis.

Structured Data

Definition: Structured data is highly organized and easily searchable in databases. It follows a predefined schema, meaning it is stored in a tabular format with rows and columns, where each column represents a different attribute or field, and each row represents a different record.

Characteristics:

- Schema-based: Adheres to a strict schema with defined data types and formats.
- Ease of Access: Easily queryable using Structured Query Language (SQL).
- Consistency: Maintains consistency and accuracy through validation rules and constraints.

Examples:

- Relational Databases: Tables in databases like MySQL, Oracle, and PostgreSQL.
- Spreadsheets: Data stored in Excel or Google Sheets.
- CSV Files: Comma-separated values files.

Use Cases:

- Business Intelligence: Analyzing sales data, customer demographics, and financial records.
- Inventory Management: Tracking stock levels, product details, and supplier information.

Unstructured Data

Definition: Unstructured data lacks a predefined format or schema, making it difficult to store and analyze using traditional relational databases. This type of data is typically text-heavy but can also include multimedia files like images, videos, and audio.

Characteristics:

- No Fixed Format: Does not conform to a specific structure or schema.
- Variety: Can include text, images, audio, video, and more.
- Complexity: Requires advanced tools and techniques for processing and analysis.

Examples:

- Text Files: Emails, Word documents, PDFs.
- Multimedia: Photos, videos, audio recordings.
- Social Media: Tweets, Facebook posts, blog entries.

Use Cases:

- Natural Language Processing (NLP): Analyzing text for sentiment, keyword extraction, and topic modeling.
- Content Management: Organizing and retrieving multimedia content.
- Social Media Analysis: Understanding trends and user behavior on social platforms.

Semi-Structured Data

Definition: Semi-structured data does not conform to a rigid schema like structured data, but it still contains tags or markers that separate data elements, making it easier to parse and analyze than unstructured data.

Characteristics:

- Flexible Schema: Data elements have some organizational properties but do not adhere to a strict structure.
- Self-Describing: Often includes metadata or tags to describe the data.
- Interoperability: Can be transformed and integrated with both structured and unstructured data systems.

Examples:

- XML Files: Extensible Markup Language files used for data interchange.
- JSON Files: JavaScript Object Notation, commonly used in web APIs.
- NoSQL Databases: Databases like MongoDB and CouchDB that store data in a semi-structured format.

Use Cases:

- Web Data Exchange: APIs exchanging data in JSON or XML format.
- Document Databases: Storing and retrieving documents with flexible data models.
- Big Data Applications: Processing and analyzing large volumes of varied data.

Overview of key algorithms: supervised, unsupervised, and reinforcement learning

1. Supervised Learning: Supervised learning involves training a model on a labeled dataset, where each input is associated with a corresponding target or output. The goal is to learn a mapping from inputs to outputs based on example input-output pairs. Some key algorithms in supervised learning include:

   o Linear Regression: A simple regression algorithm that models the relationship between one or more independent variables and a dependent variable by fitting a linear equation to the observed data.

   o Logistic Regression: A classification algorithm used to model the probability of a binary outcome based on one or more independent variables.

   o Support Vector Machines (SVM): A versatile algorithm used for both classification and regression tasks by finding the hyperplane that best separates the classes in the feature space.

   o Decision Trees: Tree-based models that recursively partition the feature space into regions, making decisions based on simple rules inferred from the data.

   o Random Forest: An ensemble learning method that constructs multiple decision trees during training and outputs the mode of the classes (classification) or the mean prediction (regression) of the individual trees.

   o Gradient Boosting Machines (GBM): An ensemble technique that builds decision trees sequentially, with each tree attempting to correct the errors made by the previous ones.

   o Neural Networks: Deep learning models composed of interconnected layers of nodes (neurons) that can learn complex patterns and relationships in the data.

2. Unsupervised Learning: Unsupervised learning involves training a model on an unlabeled dataset to uncover hidden patterns, structures, or relationships within the data. Unlike supervised learning, there are no predefined target variables to guide the learning process. Key algorithms in unsupervised learning include:

   o K-Means Clustering: A partitioning algorithm that divides the data into 'k' distinct clusters based on similarity, with each cluster represented by its centroid.

   o Hierarchical Clustering: A method that creates a hierarchy of clusters by recursively merging or dividing clusters based on their proximity.

   o Principal Component Analysis (PCA): A dimensionality reduction technique that projects high-dimensional data onto a lower-dimensional subspace while preserving the maximum variance.

   o Independent Component Analysis (ICA): A method for separating a multivariate signal into additive, statistically independent components.

   o Generative Adversarial Networks (GANs): Deep learning architectures composed of two neural networks—the generator and the discriminator—that compete against each other to generate realistic synthetic data.

3. Reinforcement Learning: Reinforcement learning involves training an agent to interact with an environment by taking actions to maximize cumulative rewards. The agent learns through trial and error, receiving feedback in the form of rewards or penalties for its actions. Key algorithms in reinforcement learning include:

   o Q-Learning: A model-free reinforcement learning algorithm that learns to make decisions by estimating the value of taking a particular action in a given state.

   o Deep Q-Networks (DQN): A deep learning variant of Q-learning that uses a neural network to approximate the Q-function, enabling the agent to handle high-dimensional state spaces.

- o Policy Gradient Methods: Algorithms that directly learn a policy function that maps states to actions, optimizing for the expected cumulative reward.

- o Actor-Critic Methods: Hybrid algorithms that combine elements of both value-based (e.g., Q-learning) and policy-based (e.g., policy gradients) methods by using separate actor and critic networks.

These key algorithms form the foundation of machine learning and are applied across various domains to solve a wide range of tasks, including classification, regression, clustering, dimensionality reduction, and sequential decision-making.

Part II: Machine Learning

Introduction to Machine Learning

Definition and Importance

Machine learning involves the use of algorithms and statistical models to analyze and draw inferences from patterns in data. It enables computers to learn from past experiences (data) and adapt their behavior accordingly. This ability to learn and improve makes machine learning incredibly powerful in handling tasks that are too complex for traditional programming methods.

The importance of machine learning lies in its versatility and effectiveness in a wide range of applications. It has transformed various industries by enabling the automation of complex tasks, providing insights from vast datasets, and creating systems that can perform tasks previously thought to require human intelligence.

Types of Machine Learning

1. Supervised Learning: In supervised learning, the algorithm is trained on a labeled dataset, meaning each training example is paired with an output label. The model learns to map inputs to the correct output based on these examples. Common applications include classification (e.g., spam detection) and regression (e.g., predicting house prices).
2. Unsupervised Learning: Unsupervised learning involves training on data without labeled responses. The goal is to infer the natural structure within a dataset. Common applications include clustering (e.g., customer segmentation) and association (e.g., market basket analysis).
3. Reinforcement Learning: In reinforcement learning, an agent learns to make decisions by performing actions and receiving feedback in the form of rewards or penalties. This type of learning is commonly used in robotics, game playing, and self-driving cars.

Key Concepts

- Training: The process of teaching a machine learning model using a dataset. The model adjusts its parameters to minimize the error in its predictions.

- Testing: Evaluating the model's performance on a separate dataset that was not used during training to ensure it can generalize to new data.
- Validation: A step between training and testing, where a portion of the training data is used to fine-tune the model parameters and select the best model.
- Overfitting: When a model performs well on training data but poorly on new, unseen data. It indicates that the model has learned noise and details in the training data that do not generalize.
- Underfitting: When a model is too simple to capture the underlying pattern in the data, leading to poor performance on both training and new data.

Common Algorithms

- Linear Regression: A method to predict a continuous target variable based on one or more input features by fitting a linear relationship.
- Decision Trees: A model that makes decisions by splitting data into subsets based on feature values, creating a tree-like structure.
- Support Vector Machines (SVM): A classification method that finds the hyperplane that best separates different classes in the feature space.
- Neural Networks: A set of algorithms modeled after the human brain, designed to recognize patterns and used in deep learning.

Applications

Machine learning has a broad range of applications across various fields:

- Healthcare: Predictive analytics for patient outcomes, personalized medicine, and medical image analysis.
- Finance: Fraud detection, algorithmic trading, and credit scoring.
- Retail: Recommendation systems, inventory management, and customer segmentation.
- Transportation: Autonomous vehicles, traffic prediction, and route optimization.
- Entertainment: Content recommendations, automated content moderation, and audience segmentation.

Machine learning is a critical component of modern AI, driving innovations and efficiencies across numerous industries. By enabling systems to learn from data, machine learning opens up possibilities for automating complex tasks, gaining insights from large datasets, and building intelligent systems that continuously improve over time. As the field evolves, its impact on technology and society will continue to grow, making it an indispensable tool for the future.

Types of machine learning

Machine learning can be broadly categorized into three main types based on the nature of the learning process and the availability of labeled data: supervised learning, unsupervised learning, and reinforcement learning.

1. Supervised Learning: Supervised learning involves training a model on a labeled dataset, where each input data point is associated with a corresponding target or output. The goal is to learn a mapping from inputs to outputs based on example input-output pairs. Supervised learning tasks can be further classified into two main types:

    o Classification: In classification tasks, the goal is to predict the category or class label of new observations based on past observations with known labels. Examples include spam detection, image recognition, sentiment analysis, and medical diagnosis.

    o Regression: In regression tasks, the goal is to predict a continuous numeric value based on input features. Examples include predicting house prices, stock prices, sales forecasts, and customer lifetime value.

Popular algorithms for supervised learning include linear regression, logistic regression, support vector machines (SVM), decision trees, random forests, gradient boosting, and neural networks.

2. Unsupervised Learning: Unsupervised learning involves training a model on an unlabeled dataset, where the algorithm tries to learn the underlying structure or patterns within the data without explicit guidance. Unsupervised learning tasks can be broadly categorized into two main types:

    o Clustering: In clustering tasks, the goal is to group similar data points together into clusters based on their intrinsic properties or similarities.

Examples include customer segmentation, document clustering, and anomaly detection.

- o Dimensionality Reduction: In dimensionality reduction tasks, the goal is to reduce the number of input variables (features) while preserving the essential information present in the data. Examples include principal component analysis (PCA), t-distributed stochastic neighbor embedding (t-SNE), and autoencoders.

Other unsupervised learning techniques include association rule mining, outlier detection, and density estimation.

3. Reinforcement Learning: Reinforcement learning involves training an agent to interact with an environment by taking actions to maximize cumulative rewards. The agent learns through trial and error, receiving feedback in the form of rewards or penalties for its actions. Reinforcement learning tasks can be characterized by the following components:

- o Agent: The entity or system that interacts with the environment and learns to make decisions.

- o Environment: The external system or environment with which the agent interacts and receives feedback.

- o Actions: The set of possible actions that the agent can take within the environment.

- o Rewards: The feedback signal provided to the agent after each action, indicating the desirability of the action taken.

Popular algorithms for reinforcement learning include Q-learning, Deep Q-Networks (DQN), policy gradient methods, and actor-critic methods.

These three types of machine learning—supervised, unsupervised, and reinforcement learning—offer different approaches to learning from data and solving a wide range of real-world problems in various domains.

Key concepts: training, testing, validation, overfitting, and underfitting

1. Training: Training is the process of teaching a machine learning model to recognize patterns, relationships, and features within a dataset. During training, the model is exposed to labeled data, where each input is associated with a corresponding target or output. The model learns to make predictions or decisions by adjusting its internal parameters based on the input-output pairs in the training data. The goal of training is to minimize the error or loss function, thereby optimizing the model's performance on unseen data.

2. Testing: Testing is the process of evaluating the performance of a trained machine learning model on a separate dataset that was not used during training. The test dataset contains new, unseen examples, allowing researchers to assess how well the model generalizes to new data. By comparing the model's predictions on the test dataset with the true labels or outcomes, researchers can measure the model's accuracy, precision, recall, and other performance metrics. Testing helps ensure that the model's performance is not overestimated and provides an estimate of how well the model will perform in real-world scenarios.

3. Validation: Validation is an additional step in the training process used to assess the performance of a model and tune its hyperparameters. During validation, a portion of the training dataset is set aside as a validation dataset, which is used to evaluate the model's performance on unseen data during training. By monitoring the model's performance on the validation dataset, researchers can identify potential issues such as overfitting or underfitting and adjust the model's hyperparameters accordingly. Validation helps ensure that the model generalizes well to new data and can make accurate predictions in real-world settings.

4. Overfitting: Overfitting occurs when a machine learning model learns to capture noise or random fluctuations in the training data, rather than the underlying patterns or relationships. As a result, the model performs well on the training data but poorly on new, unseen data. Overfitting typically occurs when the model is too complex relative to the amount of training data available or when the model is trained for too many iterations. To mitigate overfitting, researchers can use techniques such as regularization, cross-validation, and early stopping, or use simpler models that are less prone to overfitting.

5. Underfitting: Underfitting occurs when a machine learning model is too simple to capture the underlying patterns or relationships in the training data. As a result, the model performs poorly on both the training data and new, unseen data. Underfitting can occur when the model is too simple or when there is insufficient training data to learn a more complex model. To address underfitting, researchers can use more complex models, collect more training data, or engineer additional features to improve the model's performance.

In summary, training involves teaching a machine learning model to recognize patterns in data, testing evaluates the model's performance on new data, validation assesses the model's performance during training, overfitting occurs when the model learns noise in the data, and underfitting occurs when the model is too simple to capture underlying patterns. These concepts are fundamental to building accurate and reliable machine learning models.

Supervised Learning

Classification and regression

1. Classification: Classification is a supervised learning task where the goal is to categorize input data into one of several predefined classes or categories. In classification, the output variable is discrete, meaning it belongs to a specific class or category. The model learns to map input features to class labels based on the examples provided during training.

For example, consider a spam email detection system. The system is trained on a dataset of emails, where each email is labeled as either "spam" or "not spam." The input features might include the email content, sender information, and subject line. The classification model learns to distinguish between spam and non-spam emails based on these features, enabling it to predict the class label (spam or not spam) for new, unseen emails.

Common algorithms used for classification tasks include logistic regression, decision trees, random forests, support vector machines (SVM), k-nearest neighbors (KNN), and neural networks. Evaluation metrics for classification models include accuracy, precision, recall, F1-score, and area under the receiver operating characteristic curve (ROC AUC).

2. Regression: Regression is another type of supervised learning task where the goal is to predict a continuous numeric value based on input features. In regression, the output variable is continuous, meaning it can take any numerical value within a range. The model learns to approximate the relationship between input features and the continuous target variable by fitting a function to the training data.

For example, consider a real estate price prediction model. The model is trained on a dataset of houses, where each house is described by features such as size, number of bedrooms, location, and amenities. The regression model learns to predict the sale price of a house based on these features, enabling it to estimate the price of new, unseen houses.

Common algorithms used for regression tasks include linear regression, polynomial regression, decision trees, random forests, support vector regression (SVR), and neural networks. Evaluation metrics for regression models include mean squared error (MSE), root mean squared error (RMSE), mean absolute error (MAE), and R-squared coefficient.

In summary, classification and regression are two fundamental tasks in supervised learning. Classification involves categorizing input data into predefined classes or categories, while regression involves predicting a continuous numeric value based on input features. Both tasks play a crucial role in solving a wide range of real-world problems across various domains.

Common algorithms: Linear regression, Decision trees, Support Vector Machines, Neural networks

1. Linear Regression: Linear regression is a simple yet powerful algorithm used for modeling the relationship between a dependent variable (target) and one or more independent variables (features). It assumes a linear relationship between the input variables and the output variable and aims to find the best-fitting straight line (or hyperplane in higher dimensions) that minimizes the difference between the observed and predicted values.

Linear regression is widely used in various applications, including predicting house prices based on features like size, number of bedrooms, and location; forecasting sales based on marketing spending; and estimating the relationship between variables in scientific research.

2. Decision Trees: Decision trees are versatile algorithms used for both classification and regression tasks. They partition the feature space into regions based on the values of input features and make decisions by following a tree-like structure of binary splits. Each internal node represents a feature test, each branch represents a possible outcome of the test, and each leaf node represents a class label (for classification) or a predicted value (for regression).

Decision trees are intuitive, easy to interpret, and capable of capturing complex relationships in the data. They are used in applications such as customer segmentation, medical diagnosis, fraud detection, and risk assessment.

3. Support Vector Machines (SVM): Support Vector Machines (SVM) are powerful supervised learning algorithms used for classification, regression, and outlier detection tasks. SVMs aim to find the hyperplane that best separates the classes in the feature space while maximizing the margin between the classes. In cases where the data is not linearly separable, SVMs use kernel functions to map the input features into a higher-dimensional space where separation is possible.

SVMs are effective in high-dimensional spaces and are widely used in applications such as text classification, image recognition, bioinformatics, and financial forecasting.

4. Neural Networks: Neural networks are a class of algorithms inspired by the structure and function of the human brain. They consist of interconnected nodes (neurons) organized into layers, including an input layer, one or more hidden layers, and an output layer. Neural networks use a combination of linear and nonlinear transformations to learn complex patterns and relationships in the data.

Deep neural networks, with multiple hidden layers, are particularly effective for modeling complex, high-dimensional data and are used in applications such as image recognition, natural language processing, speech recognition, autonomous vehicles, and recommendation systems.

In summary, linear regression is used for modeling linear relationships between variables, decision trees provide interpretable models for classification and regression tasks, Support Vector Machines (SVM) are effective for separating classes in high-dimensional spaces, and neural networks excel at learning complex patterns and relationships in data. Each of these algorithms has its strengths and weaknesses and is suited to different types of problems and datasets.

Case studies and applications

1. Image Classification: Supervised learning is extensively used in image classification tasks, where the goal is to categorize images into predefined classes or categories. For example, in healthcare, supervised learning algorithms can be trained to classify medical images such as X-rays, MRIs, and CT scans to diagnose diseases like cancer, fractures, or abnormalities.

2. Natural Language Processing (NLP): In NLP, supervised learning algorithms are used for various tasks such as sentiment analysis, named entity recognition, part-of-speech tagging, and text classification. For instance, in customer service, supervised learning models can be trained to classify customer inquiries into different categories for routing to the appropriate department or agent.

3. Recommendation Systems: Supervised learning plays a crucial role in recommendation systems, where the goal is to predict user preferences and recommend relevant items or content. For example, in e-commerce platforms like Amazon or Netflix, supervised learning algorithms analyze user behavior and historical data to make personalized product recommendations, movie or TV show suggestions, or music recommendations.

4. Financial Fraud Detection: Supervised learning algorithms are employed in financial institutions to detect fraudulent transactions and activities. By training models on labeled data of known fraudulent and legitimate transactions, supervised learning can identify patterns indicative of fraudulent behavior, such as unusual spending patterns, account access from suspicious locations, or abnormal transaction amounts.

5. Autonomous Vehicles: In the field of autonomous vehicles, supervised learning is used for various perception tasks, such as object detection, lane detection, and pedestrian recognition. Supervised learning algorithms analyze sensor data from cameras, LiDAR, and radar to identify and classify objects in the vehicle's surroundings, enabling autonomous vehicles to make informed decisions and navigate safely.

6. Drug Discovery and Healthcare: Supervised learning algorithms are employed in drug discovery and healthcare for tasks such as drug screening, molecular modeling, and patient diagnosis. In drug discovery, supervised learning models can predict the effectiveness of potential drug compounds based on their chemical properties and biological activity. In healthcare, supervised learning algorithms analyze patient data such as symptoms, medical history, and test results to assist in disease diagnosis and treatment planning.

7. Fraud Detection: In banking and finance, supervised learning is used to detect fraudulent activities such as credit card fraud, identity theft, and money laundering. By training models on historical data containing instances of fraudulent and legitimate transactions, supervised learning algorithms can identify suspicious patterns and flag potentially fraudulent transactions for further investigation.

These case studies demonstrate the diverse applications of supervised learning in AI across various industries and domains, highlighting its ability to solve complex problems, make accurate predictions, and drive innovation and efficiency.

Unsupervised Learning

Clustering and association

1. Clustering: Clustering is a method used in unsupervised learning to group similar data points together based on their intrinsic characteristics or features. The goal of clustering is to partition the dataset into clusters or groups, where data points within the same cluster are more similar to each other than to those in other clusters. Clustering does not require labeled data, as it aims to discover the underlying structure or patterns in the data on its own.

There are various algorithms for clustering, including:

- K-Means Clustering: A popular partitioning algorithm that divides the data into 'k' clusters by minimizing the sum of squared distances between data points and their respective cluster centroids.

- Hierarchical Clustering: A method that creates a hierarchy of clusters by recursively merging or dividing clusters based on their proximity.

- DBSCAN (Density-Based Spatial Clustering of Applications with Noise): A density-based clustering algorithm that groups together data points that are closely packed, while marking outliers as noise.

- Gaussian Mixture Models (GMM): A probabilistic clustering algorithm that assumes that the data is generated from a mixture of several Gaussian distributions.

Clustering is used in various applications such as customer segmentation, image segmentation, anomaly detection, document clustering, and recommendation systems.

2. Association: Association analysis, also known as market basket analysis, is another technique in unsupervised learning used to discover interesting relationships or associations between items in a dataset. The goal of association analysis is to identify frequent patterns, correlations, or co-occurrences among items in transactional data.

Association rules are typically expressed in the form of "if-then" statements, where:

- An antecedent (or left-hand side) represents a set of items that are found together.

- A consequent (or right-hand side) represents an item that tends to occur with the items in the antecedent.

Common algorithms for association analysis include:

- Apriori Algorithm: A classical algorithm that generates association rules by iteratively discovering frequent itemsets, starting from smaller itemsets and gradually increasing their size.

- FP-Growth (Frequent Pattern Growth): An efficient algorithm that constructs a compact data structure called the FP-tree to mine frequent itemsets without generating candidate itemsets explicitly.

Association analysis is widely used in market basket analysis, cross-selling, recommendation systems, and web usage mining to uncover purchasing patterns, customer behavior, and user preferences.

Common algorithms: K-means, Hierarchical clustering, Apriori, Principal Component Analysis

1. K-means: K-means clustering is a popular partitioning algorithm used to divide a dataset into 'k' distinct clusters. The algorithm iteratively assigns data points to the nearest cluster centroid and then recalculates the centroids based on the mean of the data points assigned to each cluster. The process continues until the centroids no longer change significantly or a specified number of iterations is reached.

K-means is simple, efficient, and scalable, making it suitable for large datasets. However, it requires the number of clusters (k) to be specified in advance and is sensitive to the initial selection of centroids. K-means is widely used in applications such as customer segmentation, image compression, and anomaly detection.

2. Hierarchical Clustering: Hierarchical clustering is a method that creates a hierarchy of clusters by recursively merging or dividing clusters based on their proximity. The algorithm can be agglomerative (bottom-up) or divisive (top-down). In agglomerative clustering, each data point starts as a single-cluster, and pairs of clusters are successively merged based on their similarity until a single cluster remains. In divisive clustering, the process begins with all data points belonging to a single cluster, which is then recursively divided into smaller clusters.

Hierarchical clustering does not require the number of clusters to be specified in advance and produces a dendrogram that illustrates the hierarchical structure of the data. However, it can be computationally expensive for large datasets. Hierarchical clustering is used in applications such as taxonomy, gene expression analysis, and document clustering.

3. Apriori: Apriori is an algorithm used for association rule mining, particularly in market basket analysis. The algorithm identifies frequent itemsets—sets of items that frequently occur together in transactions—by generating candidate itemsets and pruning those that do not meet a specified support threshold. From the frequent itemsets, association rules are generated,

indicating the likelihood of the occurrence of one item given the occurrence of another.

Apriori is widely used in retail, e-commerce, and recommendation systems to uncover purchasing patterns, cross-selling opportunities, and customer behavior. However, it can be computationally expensive for large datasets due to the combinatorial explosion of itemsets.

4. Principal Component Analysis (PCA): PCA is a dimensionality reduction technique used to transform high-dimensional data into a lower-dimensional representation while preserving the maximum variance in the data. The algorithm identifies the principal components—orthogonal linear combinations of the original features—that capture the most significant variation in the data.

PCA is used for data visualization, feature extraction, and noise reduction in various applications such as image processing, signal processing, and exploratory data analysis. By reducing the dimensionality of the data, PCA simplifies subsequent analysis and visualization while retaining essential information.

Case studies and applications

1. Market Segmentation: Unsupervised learning techniques like clustering are widely used for market segmentation, where customers are grouped into segments based on similarities in their behavior, preferences, or demographics. By analyzing transactional data and customer attributes, businesses can identify distinct customer segments and tailor marketing strategies, product offerings, and pricing strategies to meet the specific needs of each segment.

2. Anomaly Detection: Anomaly detection is the identification of patterns or instances in data that deviate from normal behavior. Unsupervised learning algorithms such as clustering, density estimation, and autoencoders can be used to detect anomalies in various domains, including cybersecurity, fraud detection, manufacturing, and predictive maintenance. By identifying unusual patterns or outliers in data, organizations can proactively detect and mitigate potential issues, threats, or errors.

3. Image and Video Processing: Unsupervised learning techniques are used in image and video processing tasks such as image segmentation, object detection, and video summarization. Algorithms like K-means clustering and Gaussian mixture models (GMM) are employed to segment images into regions with similar visual characteristics, enabling tasks such as background subtraction, object tracking, and content-based image retrieval.

4. Customer Behavior Analysis: Unsupervised learning is used to analyze customer behavior and preferences in various industries, including e-commerce, retail, and digital marketing. By analyzing clickstream data, browsing history, and purchase patterns, unsupervised learning algorithms can identify common purchasing trends, recommend products or services based on past behavior, and personalize the user experience through targeted advertising, content recommendations, and email marketing campaigns.

5. Genomics and Bioinformatics: Unsupervised learning techniques play a crucial role in genomics and bioinformatics for tasks such as gene expression analysis, protein structure prediction, and clustering of biological sequences. By analyzing large-scale genomic and proteomic data,

6. unsupervised learning algorithms can identify patterns, motifs, and functional relationships among genes, proteins, and biological pathways, facilitating drug discovery, disease diagnosis, and personalized medicine.

7. Natural Language Processing (NLP): Unsupervised learning methods are used in NLP for tasks such as topic modeling, word embedding, and text clustering. Algorithms like Latent Dirichlet Allocation (LDA) and word2vec are employed to uncover latent topics in large text corpora, represent words as dense vectors in a continuous vector space, and cluster documents based on their semantic similarity. These techniques are used in applications such as document summarization, sentiment analysis, and information retrieval.

Reinforcement Learning

Basic principles

Reinforcement Learning: Basic Principles

Reinforcement Learning (RL) is a type of machine learning where an agent learns to make decisions by performing actions in an environment to maximize cumulative rewards. Unlike supervised learning, where the model is trained on a dataset with known output labels, RL involves learning through interaction and feedback from the environment. The core principles of reinforcement learning can be summarized as follows:

1. Agent and Environment:

   o Agent: The learner or decision-maker that interacts with the environment to achieve a goal.

   o Environment: The external system or domain in which the agent operates and interacts. It provides feedback in the form of rewards or punishments based on the actions taken by the agent.

2. States, Actions, and Rewards:

   o State (s): A representation of the current situation or configuration of the environment. It provides the necessary context for the agent to make decisions.

   o Action (a): A set of all possible moves or decisions the agent can make in a given state. Actions lead to transitions from one state to another.

   o Reward (r): A scalar feedback signal received by the agent after taking an action in a particular state. The reward indicates the immediate benefit or cost of the action.

3. Policy (π):

   o A policy is a strategy or mapping from states to actions that defines the agent's behavior. The policy can be deterministic (specific action for each state) or stochastic (probability distribution over actions).

4. Value Function (V) and Q-Function (Q):

   o Value Function (V): A function that estimates the expected cumulative reward of being in a given state and following a particular policy thereafter. It helps in evaluating the desirability of states.

   o Q-Function (Q): Also known as the action-value function, it estimates the expected cumulative reward of taking a particular action in a given state and following a specific policy thereafter. It helps in evaluating the desirability of state-action pairs.

5. Exploration and Exploitation:

   o Exploration: The process of trying out new actions to discover their effects and potentially find better rewards. It involves taking actions that may not be optimal based on current knowledge to gain more information about the environment.

   o Exploitation: The process of selecting actions based on the current best-known policy to maximize rewards. It involves leveraging existing knowledge to make the best possible decisions.

6. Learning Process:

   o The agent learns to improve its policy based on the feedback received from the environment. The learning process involves adjusting the policy to maximize the expected cumulative reward. Common methods for updating policies and value functions include dynamic programming, Monte Carlo methods, and temporal-difference learning.

7. Key Algorithms:

   o Q-Learning: An off-policy algorithm that aims to learn the optimal Q-function, which provides the maximum expected cumulative reward for state-action pairs.

- SARSA (State-Action-Reward-State-Action): An on-policy algorithm that updates the Q-function based on the action taken by the current policy.

- **Deep Q-Network

Deep Q-Network (DQN): A variant of Q-learning that uses deep neural networks to approximate the Q-function, allowing it to handle high-dimensional state spaces. DQN leverages techniques like experience replay and target networks to stabilize training.

Example Scenario:

To illustrate these principles, let's consider a simple example of an agent learning to play a video game, such as navigating a maze:

1. Agent and Environment:

    - Agent: The player or program trying to solve the maze.

    - Environment: The maze itself, which includes walls, paths, and a goal.

2. States, Actions, and Rewards:

    - State: The current position of the agent in the maze.

    - Action: Possible moves (up, down, left, right).

    - Reward: A positive reward for reaching the goal, negative rewards (penalties) for hitting walls, and small negative rewards for each move to encourage the agent to find the shortest path.

3. Policy (π):

    - The agent's strategy for deciding the next move based on its current position in the maze.

4. Value Function (V) and Q-Function (Q):

    - Value Function (V): Estimates how good it is to be at a certain position (state) in the maze.

- Q-Function (Q): Estimates how good it is to take a particular move (action) from a given position (state).

5. Exploration and Exploitation:

- Exploration: The agent tries different paths to discover new parts of the maze and learn about potential rewards or penalties.

- Exploitation: The agent follows the best-known path to the goal based on its current knowledge.

6. Learning Process:

- As the agent navigates the maze, it updates its policy and Q-values based on the rewards it receives. Initially, it might explore randomly, but over time, it learns to exploit the best paths it has discovered.

7. Key Algorithms:

- Q-Learning: The agent updates its Q-values based on the maximum expected future rewards.

- SARSA: The agent updates its Q-values based on the actual actions taken, following its current policy.

- DQN: The agent uses a neural network to approximate the Q-function, handling more complex mazes and larger state spaces.

Applications:

Reinforcement learning has numerous real-world applications, including:

- Game Playing: RL algorithms have been used to train agents to play and excel in games such as chess, Go, and video games like Atari and StarCraft.

- Robotics: RL helps robots learn tasks such as grasping objects, navigating environments, and performing complex manipulation tasks.

- Autonomous Vehicles: RL is used to train self-driving cars to navigate streets, avoid obstacles, and make driving decisions.

- Finance: RL algorithms are applied to optimize trading strategies, manage investment portfolios, and mitigate risks.

- Healthcare: RL is used to develop personalized treatment plans, optimize resource allocation, and enhance medical decision-making.

Key algorithms: Q-learning, Deep Q-networks, Policy gradients

Q-learning

Q-learning is a model-free reinforcement learning algorithm that aims to learn the optimal action-selection policy for any given finite Markov Decision Process (MDP). It seeks to learn the quality of actions, denoted as Q-values, which represent the expected cumulative reward of

Exploration vs. Exploitation: Q-learning balances exploration (trying new actions) and exploitation (choosing actions that maximize expected rewards) using strategies like epsilon-greedy, where a small probability ϵ\epsilon$ is used to select a random action.

Deep Q-networks (DQN)

Deep Q-networks combine Q-learning with deep neural networks to handle high-dimensional state spaces, making them suitable for complex tasks such as playing video games directly from pixel inputs.

- Neural Network: A deep neural network is used to approximate the Q-function, taking the state sss as input and producing Q-values for all possible actions.
- Experience Replay: DQN uses a replay buffer to store experiences (state, action, reward, next state) and samples mini-batches randomly during training. This breaks the correlation between consecutive experiences and stabilizes learning.
- Target Network: A separate target network is used to compute target Q-values. This network is periodically updated with the weights of the main Q-network to further stabilize training:

    Loss Function: The DQN minimizes the difference between the predicted Q-values and target Q-values using the mean squared error loss:

$$ss = E[(r + \gamma a' \max Qtarget(s', a') - Q(s, a))2]$$

Policy Gradients

Policy gradient methods directly optimize the policy by learning a parameterized policy that can select actions without relying on a value function. These methods are effective in environments with continuous action spaces and stochastic policies.

- Policy Representation: The policy $\pi\theta(a|s)$ is represented by a parameterized model (e.g., a neural network) that outputs a probability distribution over actions given a state.
- Objective Function: The goal is to maximize the expected cumulative reward, which is achieved by adjusting the policy parameters
- Policy Gradient Theorem
- REINFORCE Algorithm: A basic policy gradient algorithm that uses the Monte Carlo estimate of the return to update the policy parameters:

Summary

- Q-learning: Learns the value of actions to develop an optimal policy, using the Bellman equation for updates. It is suitable for discrete state-action spaces.
- Deep Q-networks (DQN): Extends Q-learning to handle high-dimensional state spaces with deep neural networks, using techniques like experience replay and target networks for stability.
- Policy Gradients: Directly optimize the policy without needing a value function, suitable for continuous action spaces and stochastic policies, using gradient ascent on the expected reward.

Each of these algorithms has its strengths and is suitable for different types of reinforcement learning problems, ranging from simple discrete tasks to complex continuous action environments.

Applications in gaming, robotics, and beyond

Applications in Gaming

1. Game Playing:

    o Atari Games: One of the landmark achievements in RL was using Deep Q-Networks (DQN) to play and master a range of Atari 2600 games directly from pixel inputs. The agent learned to play games like Breakout and Space Invaders at superhuman levels.

    o Chess and Go: AlphaGo, developed by DeepMind, used a combination of supervised learning and reinforcement learning to defeat the world champion Go player. Similarly, AlphaZero mastered chess, shogi, and Go through self-play and RL, achieving superhuman performance.

    o Real-time Strategy Games: RL has been applied to complex games like StarCraft II. Agents learn strategies, resource management, and tactics through millions of simulated matches, often surpassing human expertise.

2. Personalized Gaming Experience:

    o RL algorithms personalize gaming experiences by adapting game difficulty and content to individual players' skill levels and preferences, thereby enhancing user engagement and satisfaction.

Applications in Robotics

1. Autonomous Navigation:

    o Self-Driving Cars: RL is used in autonomous vehicles to learn driving policies for navigation, obstacle avoidance, and decision-making under various traffic conditions. The agents are trained using simulated environments to improve safety and efficiency.

    o Drones: RL helps in developing navigation algorithms for drones, enabling them to perform tasks such as package delivery, surveillance, and search and rescue operations in dynamic and complex environments.

2. Robotic Manipulation:

   o Grasping Objects: Robots use RL to learn how to grasp and manipulate objects with varying shapes, sizes, and weights. This involves optimizing the gripping force and positioning through trial and error.

   o Assembly Tasks: RL enables robots to learn assembly tasks, such as fitting parts together in manufacturing settings, by learning precise control and coordination.

3. Human-Robot Interaction:

   o RL is employed to enhance human-robot interaction by enabling robots to adapt their behaviors based on human feedback and preferences, improving collaboration in settings like healthcare, elderly care, and collaborative manufacturing.

Applications Beyond Gaming and Robotics

1. Healthcare:

   o Personalized Treatment Plans: RL is used to develop personalized treatment plans by optimizing medication dosages, schedules, and other treatment parameters based on patient-specific data.

   o Surgical Robots: Surgical robots equipped with RL can assist surgeons by learning optimal surgical procedures and adapting to real-time feedback during operations.

2. Finance:

   o Algorithmic Trading: RL algorithms optimize trading strategies by learning from historical market data, aiming to maximize returns while managing risks.

- o Portfolio Management: RL helps in dynamically adjusting asset allocations in investment portfolios to achieve optimal performance based on market conditions and investment goals.

3. Energy Management:

   - o Smart Grids: RL is applied to optimize the operation of smart grids, including load balancing, demand response, and energy distribution, to enhance efficiency and reliability.

   - o Building Energy Management: RL is used to optimize heating, ventilation, and air conditioning (HVAC) systems in buildings, reducing energy consumption while maintaining occupant comfort.

4. Natural Language Processing (NLP):

   - o Conversational Agents: RL improves conversational agents and chatbots by optimizing dialogue strategies to enhance user satisfaction and task completion rates.

   - o Machine Translation: RL is applied to improve the quality of machine translation systems by fine-tuning translation policies based on feedback and user interactions.

5. Supply Chain Optimization:

   - o RL is used to optimize various aspects of supply chains, including inventory management, logistics, and distribution, to reduce costs and improve efficiency.

6. Personalization and Recommendation Systems:

   - o Content Recommendations: RL algorithms personalize content recommendations on platforms like Netflix, YouTube, and Amazon by learning user preferences and optimizing recommendation policies.

   - o Advertising: RL is employed to optimize ad placements and targeting strategies to maximize engagement and conversion rates.

Part III: Deep Learning

Introduction to Deep Learning

Basics of Neural Networks

Neural networks are a class of machine learning algorithms inspired by the structure and function of the human brain. They consist of interconnected nodes, called neurons, organized into layers. These networks are capable of learning complex patterns and representations from data.

Structure of a Neural Network

1. Neurons:
   - The fundamental units of a neural network are neurons (also known as nodes or units).
   - Each neuron receives one or more inputs, processes them, and produces an output.
   - The output of a neuron is typically passed through an activation function.
2. Layers:
   - Input Layer: The first layer of the network, which receives the raw input data.
   - Hidden Layers: Layers between the input and output layers. These layers perform intermediate computations and transformations on the input data. There can be one or many hidden layers in a network.
   - Output Layer: The final layer of the network, which produces the output of the network. The number of neurons in this layer corresponds to the number of desired output variables.
3. Connections and Weights:
   - Neurons in adjacent layers are connected by links, each with an associated weight.
   - The weights determine the strength and direction of the influence of one neuron's output on another neuron's input.

Forward Propagation

Forward propagation is the process of passing input data through the network to generate an output. This involves the following steps:

1. Weighted Sum:
   - For each neuron in a layer, compute the weighted sum of its inputs

$$z = i\sum w_i x_i + b$$

Here, wi are the weight, xi are the inputs, and b is the bias term.

2. Activation Function:
    o Apply an activation function to the weighted sum to introduce non-linearity into the model:

$$a = \sigma(z)$$

Common activation functions include:

- Sigmoid: $\sigma(z) = 1 + e - z1$
- ReLU (Rectified Linear Unit): $\sigma(z) = \max(0, z)$
- Tanh: $\sigma(z) = \tanh(z)$

3. Output Calculation:
    o The output of one layer becomes the input to the next layer.
    o The final output is generated by the output layer.

Training a Neural Network

Training a neural network involves adjusting the weights and biases to minimize the difference between the predicted output and the true output. This process is called learning and is typically done using the following steps:

1. Loss Function:
    o Define a loss (or cost) function that quantifies the error between the predicted output and the true output.
    o Common loss functions include Mean Squared Error (MSE) for regression tasks and Cross-Entropy Loss for classification tasks.
2. Backward Propagation (Backpropagation):
    o Compute the gradient of the loss function with respect to each weight using the chain rule of calculus.
    o The gradients indicate how much the weights need to be adjusted to reduce the loss.
3. Gradient Descent:
    o Update the weights iteratively using gradient descent or its variants (e.g., stochastic gradient descent, Adam optimizer):

Neural networks consist of interconnected neurons organized into input, hidden, and output layers. Each neuron processes input data through weighted sums and activation functions. Forward propagation passes input data through the network to generate an output, while backward propagation adjusts weights based on the error between predicted and true outputs. Training a neural network involves iteratively updating weights to minimize the loss function using optimization techniques like gradient descent. Neural networks are powerful tools for learning complex patterns and representations, making them fundamental in many machine learning applications.

Differences Between Shallow and Deep Networks

1. Definition

- Shallow Networks:
    - A shallow network typically consists of one input layer, one hidden layer, and one output layer.
    - The hidden layer can have any number of neurons, but the network is considered shallow due to the single hidden layer.
- Deep Networks:
    - A deep network has multiple hidden layers between the input and output layers.
    - This depth allows the network to model more complex functions and representations.
    - Deep networks are often referred to as deep learning models.

2. Complexity and Representation

- Shallow Networks:
    - Can capture simpler patterns and relationships in the data.
    - With only one hidden layer, shallow networks have limited capacity to model complex functions and hierarchical representations.
    - They might struggle with tasks that require learning intricate features from the data.
- Deep Networks:
    - Capable of learning complex and hierarchical features from data.
    - Multiple layers allow deep networks to progressively build up higher-level representations from lower-level features (e.g., edges to shapes to objects in image recognition).
    - They are well-suited for tasks with significant complexity and variability, such as image and speech recognition, and natural language processing.

3. Training Requirements

- Shallow Networks:
    - Easier and faster to train compared to deep networks due to fewer layers.
    - Require fewer computational resources and are less prone to issues like vanishing gradients.

- o Suitable for smaller datasets and simpler problems.
- Deep Networks:
  - o Require more computational power and memory to train due to the larger number of parameters and layers.
  - o Often need advanced optimization techniques and regularization methods to prevent overfitting and issues like vanishing/exploding gradients.
  - o Beneficial for large datasets and complex problems where the depth of the model can be fully leveraged.

4. Generalization

- Shallow Networks:
  - o May generalize well for simpler tasks or problems with low-dimensional feature spaces.
  - o Risk of underfitting on complex tasks because they cannot model intricate patterns adequately.
- Deep Networks:
  - o Tend to generalize better on complex tasks if trained properly, thanks to their ability to learn detailed and abstract features.
  - o However, they are also at risk of overfitting, especially with limited data, requiring techniques like dropout, data augmentation, and regularization to improve generalization.

5. Applications

- Shallow Networks:
  - o Suitable for tasks where the relationships in the data can be captured with a single layer of transformation, such as basic regression, simple classification problems, or signal processing.
  - o Commonly used in scenarios where computational efficiency and simplicity are crucial.
- Deep Networks:
  - o Ideal for tasks requiring deep feature extraction and high-level abstraction, including image classification, object detection, natural language processing, and complex game playing.
  - o Employed in cutting-edge applications like autonomous driving, advanced robotics, and personalized recommendation systems.

6. Model Interpretability

- Shallow Networks:
  - Generally more interpretable because of their simpler structure and fewer layers.
  - Easier to understand how input features contribute to the output.
- Deep Networks:
  - Often less interpretable due to their complex, multi-layered structure.
  - The decision-making process is more opaque, making it challenging to trace how specific input features affect the output.

Importance of Deep Learning

Deep learning, a subset of machine learning, has revolutionized the field of artificial intelligence (AI) over the past decade. It leverages neural networks with multiple layers (deep networks) to model complex patterns in data. The significance of deep learning spans across various domains and applications, fundamentally transforming technology and society.

Key Reasons for the Importance of Deep Learning

1. Ability to Handle Complex Data:
    o Feature Learning: Deep learning models automatically learn and extract hierarchical features from raw data. Unlike traditional machine learning, which often requires manual feature engineering, deep networks can discover intricate patterns directly from the data.
    o Multimodal Data: Deep learning excels in processing and integrating various data types, including images, text, audio, and video, enabling comprehensive understanding and analysis in applications like multimedia and social media.

2. Superior Performance in Critical Applications:
    o Image and Video Analysis: Convolutional Neural Networks (CNNs), a type of deep learning model, have set new benchmarks in tasks such as image classification, object detection, and video analysis. Applications include medical imaging, autonomous driving, and surveillance.
    o Natural Language Processing (NLP): Recurrent Neural Networks (RNNs) and Transformers have significantly advanced NLP tasks like machine translation, sentiment analysis, and chatbots. They enable more accurate and fluent interactions in human language.
    o Speech Recognition: Deep learning models have drastically improved the accuracy of speech recognition systems, leading to more reliable voice assistants and transcription services.

3. Scalability and Adaptability:

- Large-Scale Data Handling: Deep learning models are designed to handle vast amounts of data, leveraging massive datasets to learn more accurately and comprehensively. This capability is crucial in domains like genomics, where large datasets are the norm.
- Transfer Learning: Deep learning allows models trained on large datasets to be fine-tuned for specific tasks with smaller datasets, enabling quick adaptation and deployment in various applications.

4. Advancements in Technology and Innovation:
   - Autonomous Systems: Deep learning is integral to the development of autonomous systems, such as self-driving cars and drones. These systems rely on deep learning for tasks like perception, decision-making, and control.
   - Healthcare and Medical Research: Deep learning aids in disease diagnosis, drug discovery, and personalized medicine by analyzing complex biomedical data, leading to improved healthcare outcomes.
   - Robotics: Deep learning enables robots to perform complex tasks such as object manipulation, navigation, and human-robot interaction, advancing automation in industries and homes.

5. Enhanced Accuracy and Efficiency:
   - Higher Precision: Deep learning models often surpass traditional methods in accuracy for tasks like image recognition and language understanding, making them preferable for applications where precision is critical.
   - Efficiency in Learning: Deep learning models can efficiently learn from massive amounts of data, continuously improving their performance as more data becomes available.

6. Empowering AI Research and Development:
   - Foundation for AI: Deep learning is a cornerstone of modern AI research, driving advancements in fields like computer vision, NLP, and robotics. It provides a robust framework for developing intelligent systems that can perceive, reason, and act.

- Innovation Driver: The flexibility and power of deep learning models foster innovation, leading to new AI applications and capabilities that were previously unattainable with traditional machine learning approaches.

7. Impact on Society and Industry:
   - Economic Transformation: Deep learning is reshaping industries by automating processes, enhancing productivity, and enabling new business models. Sectors such as finance, retail, and manufacturing are experiencing significant transformations driven by deep learning technologies.
   - Societal Benefits: Deep learning applications are improving quality of life through innovations in healthcare, education, and public safety, making technology more accessible and beneficial to a broader population.

8. Continuous Improvement and Future Potential:
   - Ongoing Research: Deep learning continues to evolve with advancements in architectures, algorithms, and computational techniques, pushing the boundaries of what AI systems can achieve.
   - Future Prospects: The potential of deep learning extends to emerging fields like quantum computing, augmented reality, and climate science, promising breakthroughs that can address global challenges and enhance human capabilities.

Deep Learning Architectures

Convolutional Neural Networks (CNNs)

Convolutional Neural Networks (CNNs) are a specialized type of neural network designed for processing structured grid data, such as images. CNNs have revolutionized the field of computer vision and are widely used for tasks like image classification, object detection, and image generation. Their architecture is inspired by the visual cortex of animals, which processes visual information in a hierarchical manner.

Key Components and Architecture of CNNs

1. Convolutional Layers:
   - Convolution Operation: The core component of CNNs is the convolutional layer, which applies a set of learnable filters (also called kernels) to the input data. Each filter convolves across the input, producing a feature map that highlights specific features such as edges, textures, or shapes.
   - Filters and Feature Maps: Filters are small matrices that slide over the input data. Each filter detects a particular pattern, and the output of applying a filter is a feature map that captures the spatial characteristics of the input.
   - Stride and Padding: Stride determines the step size by which the filter moves over the input. Padding adds extra pixels around the input to control the spatial dimensions of the output feature map, allowing for better edge handling and control over the feature map size.

2. Activation Functions:
   - After the convolution operation, an activation function, typically ReLU (Rectified Linear Unit), is applied to introduce non-linearity into the model. ReLU replaces negative values with zero, which helps in learning complex patterns by breaking linearity.
   - Other activation functions like Sigmoid or Tanh can also be used, but ReLU is preferred for its simplicity and efficiency.

3. Pooling Layers:

- o Purpose: Pooling layers are used to reduce the spatial dimensions (width and height) of the feature maps while retaining the important information. This helps in reducing the computational load and controlling overfitting.
- o Types of Pooling:
    - Max Pooling: Takes the maximum value from each patch of the feature map. It effectively captures the most prominent features and is widely used in CNNs.
    - Average Pooling: Takes the average value from each patch, providing a smoother version of the feature map.
- o Stride in Pooling: Similar to convolution, the pooling operation uses a stride to move the pooling window across the feature map.

4. Fully Connected (Dense) Layers:
    - o After several convolutional and pooling layers, the network typically includes one or more fully connected layers.
    - o These layers flatten the feature maps into a vector and perform high-level reasoning, combining the spatial features into the final output.
    - o Fully connected layers are essential for tasks like classification, where the output needs to be a probability distribution over class labels.

5. Output Layer:
    - o The final layer in a CNN is often a fully connected layer with a softmax activation function for classification tasks. This produces a probability distribution over the possible output classes.
    - o For regression tasks, the output layer might use a linear activation function to predict continuous values.

Key Characteristics of CNNs

1. Local Receptive Fields:
    - o Convolutional layers have local receptive fields, meaning that each neuron is connected to only a small region of the input. This allows the network to focus on local patterns and spatial hierarchies, making it particularly effective for image and video data.

2. Parameter Sharing:
    - In CNNs, the same filter is applied across different positions in the input, meaning the same weights are used for multiple connections. This significantly reduces the number of parameters compared to fully connected networks and helps in capturing spatially invariant features.

3. Spatial Hierarchies:
    - CNNs can build complex spatial hierarchies by stacking multiple convolutional and pooling layers. Early layers detect simple features like edges and textures, while deeper layers capture more complex structures and patterns.

4. Translation Invariance:
    - Due to the nature of convolution and pooling operations, CNNs are inherently translation invariant. This means they can recognize objects regardless of their position within the input frame, making them robust to translations in the input.

Applications of CNNs

1. Image Classification:
    - CNNs are the backbone of image classification tasks. They are used to categorize images into predefined classes, such as identifying objects in photographs or recognizing handwritten digits.
2. Object Detection:
    - Beyond classification, CNNs are used in object detection tasks, where the goal is to identify and locate multiple objects within an image. Techniques like Region-based CNN (R-CNN) and YOLO (You Only Look Once) leverage CNNs for real-time object detection.
3. Image Segmentation:
    - In image segmentation, CNNs are used to label each pixel in an image, effectively partitioning the image into meaningful segments. Applications include medical image analysis, autonomous driving, and scene understanding.
4. Video Analysis:

- CNNs extend to video analysis by processing frames to recognize activities, actions, and objects over time. They are used in applications like video surveillance, sports analytics, and entertainment.
5. Facial Recognition:
   - CNNs are widely employed in facial recognition systems to detect and identify faces in images and videos, used in security, authentication, and social media tagging.
6. Generative Modeling:
   - Variants of CNNs, like Generative Adversarial Networks (GANs), are used to generate new images that resemble the training data. GANs have applications in image synthesis, style transfer, and data augmentation.
7. Medical Imaging:
   - CNNs assist in analyzing medical images, such as X-rays, MRIs, and CT scans, to detect and diagnose diseases, tumors, and anomalies. They play a crucial role in enhancing diagnostic accuracy and speed.

Recurrent Neural Networks (RNNs)

Recurrent Neural Networks (RNNs) are a class of neural networks designed for sequential data processing. Unlike traditional feedforward neural networks, RNNs have loops in their architecture, enabling them to maintain information across different steps in the input sequence. This capability makes RNNs well-suited for tasks involving time series, natural language processing, and any data where the order and context of the elements are important.

Key Characteristics of RNNs

1. Sequential Data Handling:
   - RNNs are specifically designed to work with sequential data, where the current state is influenced by the previous inputs. This is achieved through their internal memory, which captures the context from prior steps in the sequence.
   - This makes RNNs ideal for tasks like language modeling, speech recognition, and time series prediction, where the temporal or sequential relationship is crucial.
2. Recurrent Connections:

- o In an RNN, each neuron in a layer is connected not only to the neurons in the next layer but also back to itself (recurrent connections). This feedback loop allows the network to maintain a memory of previous inputs.
- o Mathematically, at each time step t, the hidden state ht is updated based on the input xt and the previous hidden state ht-1

$$ht = f(W \cdot xt + U \cdot ht - 1 + b)$$

Here, W, U, and b are weight matrices and bias terms, and f is an activation function like ReLU.

3. Shared Parameters:
   - o The weights W, U, and biases b are shared across all time steps, allowing the RNN to generalize across different positions in the sequence. This parameter sharing reduces the number of parameters to train and enables the network to apply the same transformation to each input in the sequence.

Variants of RNNs

1. Standard RNNs:
   - o These are the basic form of RNNs, where the hidden state at each time step is passed to the next step. While they can capture dependencies, they often struggle with long-term dependencies due to issues like vanishing gradients during training.
2. Long Short-Term Memory (LSTM) Networks:
   - o LSTMs are a special type of RNN designed to handle long-term dependencies more effectively. They use a more complex architecture involving gates (input, forget, and output gates) to control the flow of information and maintain a more robust memory.
   - o The gates help LSTMs to remember important information for long periods and forget irrelevant information, making them particularly effective for tasks involving long sequences.
3. Gated Recurrent Unit (GRU) Networks:
   - o GRUs are a simplified version of LSTMs with fewer gates (update and reset gates). They combine the cell state and hidden state into a single vector, reducing complexity while still handling long-term dependencies efficiently.

- o GRUs are often used as a lightweight alternative to LSTMs with comparable performance in many applications.
4. Bidirectional RNNs:
   - o Bidirectional RNNs process the input sequence in both forward and backward directions, using two separate hidden layers. This allows the network to have a complete context from both past and future inputs, improving performance in tasks where future context is relevant, like language translation and named entity recognition.

Applications of RNNs

1. Natural Language Processing (NLP):
   - o Language Modeling: RNNs are used to predict the next word in a sentence, which is foundational for text generation, autocomplete, and machine translation.
   - o Speech Recognition: They convert speech signals into text by processing sequences of audio frames and capturing temporal dependencies in spoken language.
   - o Machine Translation: RNNs are used to translate text from one language to another by encoding the source sentence into a context vector and decoding it into the target language.
   - o Text Classification: They classify sequences of text for sentiment analysis, spam detection, and topic categorization.
2. Time Series Prediction:
   - o RNNs predict future values in a time series based on historical data. Applications include stock price forecasting, weather prediction, and energy demand forecasting.
   - o They capture temporal dependencies and trends in the data, providing more accurate predictions.
3. Sequence-to-Sequence Learning:
   - o Sequence Transduction: RNNs convert one sequence into another, such as converting an audio signal into text or generating a caption for an image.
   - o Video Analysis: They analyze video frames to recognize activities, gestures, and events by capturing temporal dynamics over time.
4. Anomaly Detection:
   - o RNNs are used to detect unusual patterns in sequential data, such as identifying fraudulent transactions, monitoring network traffic for intrusions, and detecting equipment failures in predictive maintenance.

5. Recommendation Systems:
   - RNNs enhance recommendation systems by understanding the sequence of user interactions, providing personalized recommendations based on the order and context of previous actions.

Challenges and Considerations

1. Training Difficulties:
   - Vanishing and Exploding Gradients: Standard RNNs can struggle with training over long sequences due to gradients either vanishing (becoming too small) or exploding (becoming too large). LSTMs and GRUs address these issues with their gating mechanisms.
   - Long-Term Dependencies: While RNNs can capture short-term dependencies well, they may have difficulty learning long-term dependencies. Advanced architectures like LSTMs and GRUs are better suited for such tasks.
2. Computational Complexity:
   - RNNs can be computationally intensive, especially with long sequences, due to their recurrent nature and the need to process each step sequentially.
   - Training can be slow and resource-intensive, particularly for large datasets and complex models.
3. Parallelization:
   - Unlike feedforward networks and CNNs, RNNs are challenging to parallelize due to their sequential processing, which can limit their scalability and efficiency on modern hardware architectures.
4. Architecture and Hyperparameter Tuning:
   - Designing and tuning RNNs involve selecting the appropriate architecture (e.g., standard RNN, LSTM, GRU), number of layers, hidden units, and learning rates. These choices significantly impact model performance and require careful experimentation.

Generative Adversarial Networks (GANs)

Generative Adversarial Networks (GANs) are a class of machine learning frameworks designed to generate new, synthetic data samples that resemble a given set of training data. Introduced by Ian Goodfellow and colleagues in 2014, GANs have become a foundational tool in generative modeling, significantly impacting fields such as computer vision, natural language processing, and art generation.

Core Concept of GANs

At the heart of GANs is the idea of adversarial training, where two neural networks, the Generator and the Discriminator, are pitted against each other in a zero-sum game. Their interplay drives the system to generate increasingly realistic data.

1. Generator:
   - The Generator creates new data samples from random noise. Its goal is to produce samples that are indistinguishable from the real data.
   - It starts with a random input, typically a noise vector sampled from a standard distribution (e.g., Gaussian or uniform), and transforms it through several layers into a synthetic data point, such as an image.
2. Discriminator:
   - The Discriminator evaluates the authenticity of data samples, distinguishing between real samples (from the training data) and fake samples (from the Generator).
   - It is a binary classifier that outputs a probability score indicating whether a given input is real or fake.

The Generator and Discriminator engage in a continuous battle:

- The Generator tries to fool the Discriminator by producing more realistic samples.
- The Discriminator tries to get better at detecting fake samples.

This adversarial process forces the Generator to improve its output quality until the generated samples are indistinguishable from the real data.

Training Process

The training of GANs involves optimizing two competing objectives simultaneously:

1. Discriminator Objective: To maximize the accuracy of distinguishing real data from fake data.
2. Generator Objective: To minimize the Discriminator's ability to tell the difference between real and fake data, effectively fooling the Discriminator.

The training alternates between:

- Updating the Discriminator to maximize its ability to distinguish real from fake samples.
- Updating the Generator to minimize the Discriminator's performance, thus improving the realism of generated samples.

Variants of GANs

1. Deep Convolutional GANs (DCGANs):
   - DCGANs apply convolutional layers in the Generator and Discriminator, improving the generation of high-quality images. They leverage architectural innovations from Convolutional Neural Networks (CNNs) to better handle image data.
2. Conditional GANs (cGANs):
   - cGANs incorporate additional information, such as class labels or attributes, into the Generator and Discriminator. This allows for controlled generation of samples based on specified conditions, like generating images of a specific type (e.g., dogs, cats).
3. CycleGANs:
   - CycleGANs are designed for image-to-image translation tasks without paired training examples. They enable transformations between two image domains, such as turning summer scenes into winter ones or converting photos into paintings, by learning a mapping between the domains.
4. StyleGANs:
   - StyleGANs focus on generating high-resolution images with controllable style variations. They introduce a novel approach to controlling the style of generated images at different levels of

abstraction, leading to impressive results in face generation and image synthesis.

5. Wasserstein GANs (WGANs):
   o WGANs modify the GAN objective to use the Wasserstein distance, a measure of distribution difference. This approach provides more stable training and helps address issues like mode collapse, where the Generator produces limited diversity in samples.

Applications of GANs

1. Image Generation and Enhancement:
   o Photo-realistic Image Synthesis: GANs can generate highly realistic images that are indistinguishable from real photos. This has applications in creating synthetic data for training other models, digital art, and entertainment.
   o Super-Resolution: GANs enhance the resolution of images, making low-quality images clearer and more detailed. This is useful in medical imaging, surveillance, and any field requiring detailed image analysis.

2. Data Augmentation:
   o GANs generate additional data samples to augment training datasets, especially in domains where data is scarce or expensive to obtain. This helps improve the robustness and performance of machine learning models.

3. Style Transfer and Image Translation:
   o GANs can transform images from one style to another, such as converting photos into paintings, changing day scenes to night, or translating sketches into realistic images. This is valuable in artistic applications, virtual reality, and content creation.

4. Video and Motion Synthesis:
   o GANs generate realistic video sequences and animate still images. Applications include creating synthetic videos for training autonomous systems, generating realistic animations, and enhancing video quality.

5. Text-to-Image Synthesis:
   o GANs can generate images based on textual descriptions, enabling applications like creating visual content from narrative text, assisting in creative processes, and aiding in design automation.

6. Medical Imaging:

- GANs improve medical imaging by generating high-quality images from low-resolution scans, augmenting training data for diagnostic models, and creating synthetic medical images for research and training.

7. Anomaly Detection:
   - GANs are used to detect anomalies by learning to generate typical data samples. Deviations from these generated samples can be flagged as anomalies, useful in fields like fraud detection, network security, and quality control.

Challenges and Considerations

1. Training Instability:
   - GANs can be difficult to train due to their adversarial nature. The balance between the Generator and Discriminator must be carefully managed to avoid issues like mode collapse (where the Generator produces limited diversity) or vanishing gradients (where the Discriminator becomes too strong).

2. Evaluation Metrics:
   - Evaluating the quality of generated samples is challenging. Unlike traditional supervised learning, there is no straightforward loss function to measure the performance of GANs. Metrics like Inception Score (IS), Fréchet Inception Distance (FID), and visual inspection are commonly used.

3. Computational Resources:
   - Training GANs, especially for high-resolution image generation, requires significant computational power and memory. Efficient training and optimization are essential to manage these demands.

4. Ethical Considerations:
   - The ability of GANs to generate realistic synthetic data raises ethical concerns. This includes potential misuse in creating deepfakes (realistic fake videos or images), data privacy issues, and the impact on creative industries.

Transformers in Deep Learning Architectures

Transformers are a groundbreaking architecture in deep learning that have revolutionized the field of natural language processing (NLP) and are making significant strides in various other domains. Introduced by Vaswani et al. in the 2017 paper "Attention is All You Need," transformers address the limitations of previous models like RNNs and CNNs in handling long-range dependencies and sequential data effectively.

Core Concepts of Transformers

1. Attention Mechanism:
   - At the heart of the Transformer architecture is the self-attention mechanism, which allows the model to weigh the importance of different parts of the input sequence dynamically.
   - Self-Attention: For each word in a sentence, self-attention computes a weighted sum of all the words in the sentence, allowing the model to focus on relevant words regardless of their position. This is crucial for capturing context and relationships in the data.
   - Multi-Head Attention: Transformers use multiple attention heads to capture different aspects of relationships in the data simultaneously. Each head processes the input independently, and their outputs are combined to provide a richer representation.
2. Positional Encoding:
   - Unlike RNNs and CNNs, transformers do not inherently understand the order of input sequences. To encode positional information, they add positional encodings to the input embeddings.
   - Positional encodings provide the model with information about the position of each word in the sequence, enabling it to utilize both the content and the order of the input effectively.
3. Layered Architecture:
   - Transformers consist of multiple layers of encoders and decoders, each comprising attention mechanisms and feed-forward networks.
   - Encoder: The encoder processes the input sequence and generates a contextual representation. It is composed of a stack of identical layers, each containing a self-attention mechanism and a feed-forward neural network.
   - Decoder: The decoder generates the output sequence based on the encoder's representation and previous outputs. It also consists of

multiple layers, each with self-attention, encoder-decoder attention, and a feed-forward network.

4. Feed-Forward Networks:
   - Each encoder and decoder layer contains a fully connected feed-forward network that processes the output of the attention mechanisms. This network consists of two linear transformations with a ReLU activation in between, enabling non-linear transformations of the data.

5. Normalization and Residual Connections:
   - Transformers use layer normalization and residual connections to stabilize training and improve convergence. Residual connections add the input of a layer to its output, ensuring gradient flow and helping with deeper architectures.

Transformer Architecture Overview

1. Encoder:
   - Each encoder layer applies self-attention to focus on different parts of the input sequence and uses feed-forward networks to transform these representations. The encoder's final output is a rich representation of the input sequence, capturing both local and global dependencies.

2. Decoder:
   - The decoder generates the output sequence by attending to the encoder's representations and the previously generated tokens. Each decoder layer applies self-attention to the previous outputs and cross-attention to the encoder's outputs, combining these with feed-forward transformations.

3. Output Generation:
   - The final layer of the decoder produces logits that are passed through a softmax function to generate the probability distribution over the target vocabulary, enabling sequence generation in tasks like translation or text generation.

Key Advantages of Transformers

1. Parallelization:
   - Unlike RNNs, which process sequences step-by-step, transformers allow parallel processing of input sequences due to their non-recurrent nature. This significantly speeds up training and inference, making transformers highly scalable and efficient for large datasets.

2. Long-Range Dependencies:
   - Transformers excel at capturing long-range dependencies in sequences, thanks to their attention mechanism. They can directly attend to relevant parts of the input regardless of distance, addressing the limitations of RNNs, which struggle with long-term dependencies.
3. Versatility:
   - While originally designed for NLP, transformers have been successfully applied to a wide range of tasks, including image processing, speech recognition, and even reinforcement learning. Their ability to model complex relationships makes them adaptable to various domains.
4. Scalability:
   - Transformers can scale to very large models, such as GPT-3 and BERT, by increasing the number of layers and attention heads. This scaling capability allows transformers to learn from vast amounts of data and capture intricate patterns and knowledge.

Applications of Transformers

1. Natural Language Processing (NLP):
   - Machine Translation: Transformers have set new benchmarks in translating text between languages, outperforming traditional models with their ability to handle long sentences and context effectively.
   - Text Summarization: They generate concise summaries of long documents by understanding and extracting key information from the text.
   - Question Answering: Models like BERT and GPT-3, based on transformers, excel in understanding and answering questions posed in natural language.
   - Text Generation: Transformers are used in generating coherent and contextually relevant text, as seen in applications like chatbots and content creation.
2. Image Processing:
   - Vision Transformers (ViTs): Transformers have been adapted for image tasks, treating patches of images as sequences and applying self-attention to capture spatial relationships. ViTs have shown competitive performance in image classification and segmentation tasks.

- Image Captioning: Combining CNNs for feature extraction with transformers for sequence modeling enables the generation of descriptive captions for images.
3. Speech Processing:
   - Transformers are used in automatic speech recognition (ASR) systems to transcribe spoken language into text, and in text-to-speech (TTS) systems to generate natural-sounding speech from text.
   - Their ability to handle sequences and context makes them suitable for capturing nuances in speech and language.
4. Reinforcement Learning:
   - Transformers are applied in reinforcement learning to model environments and predict future states, enhancing decision-making processes in complex tasks like gaming and robotics.
5. Biomedical and Scientific Research:
   - Transformers are employed to analyze sequences in genomics and protein structures, aiding in tasks like gene prediction and drug discovery.
   - Their capacity to model sequential data extends to understanding and generating scientific texts and papers.

Challenges and Considerations

1. Computational Cost:
   - Transformers are computationally intensive, especially for large-scale models with many layers and attention heads. Training such models requires significant resources and time, which can be a barrier for smaller organizations or research groups.
2. Data Requirements:
   - Large transformer models often require massive amounts of data to achieve their full potential. This poses a challenge in domains with limited data availability or in applications where collecting large datasets is impractical.
3. Model Size and Complexity:
   - The sheer size and complexity of transformer models can lead to difficulties in deployment and integration into systems, particularly for real-time applications with resource constraints.
4. Interpretability:
   - While transformers are powerful, their decision-making process is often opaque, making it hard to interpret why they make certain

predictions. This lack of transparency can be a drawback in applications requiring explainable AI.

5. Ethical and Societal Impact:
   - o The powerful capabilities of transformers raise ethical concerns, such as their potential use in generating misinformation, bias in language models, and the environmental impact of training large models.

Transformers represent a transformative advancement in deep learning, particularly for sequential and structured data processing. Their self-attention mechanism, ability to parallelize processing, and scalability have made them the go-to architecture for many modern AI tasks. From revolutionizing NLP with models like BERT and GPT to expanding their reach into image, speech, and scientific domains, transformers continue to push the boundaries of what AI can achieve. Despite challenges in computational demands and interpretability, their versatility and power make them a cornerstone of current and future deep learning innovations.

Training Deep Learning Models

Data Preprocessing and Augmentation

In deep learning, the preparation of data is as crucial as the design of the model itself. Properly preprocessed and augmented data can significantly enhance the performance and generalization of deep learning models. Let's explore these two essential processes: data preprocessing and data augmentation.

Data Preprocessing

Data preprocessing involves converting raw data into a clean, structured, and meaningful format for training a deep learning model. This step ensures that the data is consistent, devoid of noise, and formatted correctly, which is critical for efficient and accurate model training.

Key Steps in Data Preprocessing

1. Data Cleaning:
   o Handling Missing Values: Missing values in a dataset can hinder model performance. Several strategies can be used to address this issue:
      ▪ Imputation: Replacing missing values with statistical metrics such as the mean, median, or mode.
      ▪ Interpolation: Using algorithms to estimate missing values based on the known values.
      ▪ Dropping: Removing rows or columns with missing values if they constitute a small portion of the dataset and are unlikely to impact results significantly.
   o Removing Duplicates: Duplicates can bias the learning process by over-representing certain samples. Identifying and removing duplicate entries ensures a unique and representative dataset.
   o Outlier Detection and Handling: Outliers can skew model predictions. Techniques to handle outliers include:
      ▪ Clipping: Setting a maximum threshold to limit extreme values.
      ▪ Transformation: Applying mathematical transformations (e.g., log transformation) to reduce the impact of outliers.
      ▪ Exclusion: Directly removing outliers from the dataset if they are deemed to be noise.

2. Data Transformation:
   o Normalization and Standardization:
     ▪ Normalization scales data to a fixed range, typically [0, 1], making it suitable for algorithms sensitive to the magnitude of features.
     ▪ Standardization transforms data to have zero mean and unit variance, ensuring that features contribute equally to the model's performance.
   o Encoding Categorical Data:
     ▪ One-Hot Encoding: Converts categorical variables into binary vectors, with each category represented by a distinct bit.
     ▪ Label Encoding: Assigns unique integers to each category, useful for ordinal data but can introduce artificial relationships if used improperly.
     ▪ Embeddings: Creates dense, continuous representations for categorical features, especially useful in large-scale or deep learning models.
   o Feature Engineering:
     ▪ Creating new features from existing ones to provide more information to the model. Examples include extracting date components from timestamps or creating interaction terms between variables.
3. Dimensionality Reduction:
   o Reducing the number of features in the dataset while retaining essential information. Methods include:
     ▪ Principal Component Analysis (PCA): Projects data into a lower-dimensional space to reduce complexity and improve training speed.
     ▪ t-Distributed Stochastic Neighbor Embedding (t-SNE): Primarily used for visualization by reducing dimensions in a way that preserves the local structure of data.
4. Data Splitting:
   o Dividing the dataset into separate subsets for training, validation, and testing to evaluate model performance effectively. A typical split might be:
     ▪ Training Set: 70-80% of the data used to train the model.
     ▪ Validation Set: 10-15% of the data used to tune model parameters and prevent overfitting.
     ▪ Test Set: 10-15% of the data used for final evaluation to assess model performance on unseen data.

Data Augmentation

Data augmentation is the process of generating new training samples from the existing data to enhance model robustness and prevent overfitting. This technique is particularly beneficial when the available data is limited or imbalanced.

Common Techniques in Data Augmentation

1. Image Data Augmentation:
   - Geometric Transformations:
     - Rotation: Rotating images to various angles to simulate different viewing perspectives.
     - Translation: Shifting images horizontally or vertically to mimic changes in position.
     - Scaling: Zooming in or out to simulate different distances.
     - Flipping: Mirroring images horizontally or vertically

Loss Functions and Optimization in Training Deep Learning Models

In deep learning, loss functions and optimization are fundamental components that guide the training process. They work together to enable the model to learn from data by iteratively improving its performance on a given task.

Loss Functions

A loss function, also known as a cost function or objective function, quantifies how well a model's predictions match the actual data. It provides a measure of the difference between the predicted output and the actual target values. The goal of training is to minimize this loss function, thereby improving the model's performance.

Types of Loss Functions

1. Mean Squared Error (MSE):
   o Interpretation: MSE measures the average squared difference between the predicted and actual values. A lower MSE indicates a closer fit to the data.
2. Cross-Entropy Loss:
   o Usage: Widely used in classification tasks.
   o Interpretation: Cross-entropy loss measures the performance of a classification model whose output is a probability value between 0 and 1. It penalizes the probability assigned to the wrong class, making it effective for classification problems.
3. Binary Cross-Entropy Loss:
   o Usage: Used specifically for binary classification problems.
   o Interpretation: This loss function calculates the difference between the true labels and the predicted probabilities in binary classification tasks, encouraging the model to assign high probabilities to the correct class.
4. Categorical Cross-Entropy Loss:
   o Usage: Used for multi-class classification problems.

- Interpretation: It calculates the divergence between the true class labels and the predicted probabilities, encouraging the model to accurately predict the correct class out of multiple possible classes.

5. Huber Loss:
   - Usage: Used in regression tasks that are sensitive to outliers.
   - Interpretation: Huber loss is less sensitive to outliers in data than squared error loss and is differentiable everywhere, combining the advantages of both MSE and MAE (Mean Absolute Error).

6. Kullback-Leibler Divergence (KL Divergence):
   - Usage: Used in problems involving probability distributions, such as variational autoencoders.
   - Interpretation: KL Divergence measures how one probability distribution diverges from a second, expected probability distribution. It's useful in contexts where the goal is to make one distribution resemble another.

Optimization

Optimization algorithms are methods used to minimize or maximize the loss function. They adjust the parameters of the model to find the values that minimize the loss. The choice of optimization algorithm can significantly affect the speed and quality of the training process.

Common Optimization Algorithms

1. Gradient Descent:
   - Concept: Gradient descent is the most fundamental optimization algorithm, used to minimize a function by iteratively moving in the direction of the steepest descent as defined by the negative of the gradient.
   - Variants:
     - Batch Gradient Descent: Uses the entire dataset to compute the gradient of the loss function.
     - Stochastic Gradient Descent (SGD): Uses a single sample to compute the gradient, which makes it faster but introduces more noise in the updates.
     - Mini-Batch Gradient Descent: A compromise between batch and stochastic gradient descent, using a small random subset of the data to compute the gradient.

2. Momentum:

- o Concept: Momentum accelerates gradient descent by taking into account the past gradients to smooth out updates. It helps avoid oscillations and can lead to faster convergence.
3. RMSprop (Root Mean Square Propagation):
    - o Concept: RMSprop adapts the learning rate for each parameter by dividing the gradient by a running average of the magnitudes of recent gradients, effectively dampening the effect of large gradients.
4. Adam (Adaptive Moment Estimation):
    - o Concept: Adam combines the benefits of both momentum and RMSprop. It maintains separate learning rates for each parameter and adjusts them based on the moving averages of the gradient and its square.
5. Nesterov Accelerated Gradient (NAG):
    - o Concept: NAG improves upon momentum by making a corrective step ahead in the direction of the gradient, which leads to faster convergence.

Loss functions provide a way to quantify the error between a model's predictions and the actual values, guiding the optimization process. Optimization algorithms then use this feedback to adjust the model's parameters in a way that reduces the loss, improving the model's performance over time. Together, they form the core mechanisms that enable deep learning models to learn and adapt from data.

Addressing Challenges: Overfitting and Vanishing Gradients

Training deep learning models is a complex process that involves navigating several challenges to achieve robust and generalizable performance. Two of the most significant challenges are overfitting and vanishing gradients. Understanding these issues and employing strategies to mitigate them are crucial for developing effective deep learning models.

Overfitting

Overfitting occurs when a model learns not only the underlying patterns in the training data but also the noise and outliers. This results in excellent performance on the training data but poor generalization to new, unseen data. Essentially, the model becomes too tailored to the training dataset and fails to perform well on other datasets.

Causes of Overfitting

1. Complex Models:
    o Models with too many parameters or high complexity can capture noise and subtle anomalies in the training data, leading to overfitting.
2. Insufficient Training Data:
    o When there isn't enough data, the model may learn noise and specific details that do not generalize to a broader dataset.
3. Training for Too Long:
    o Prolonged training can cause the model to adapt too closely to the training data, especially when combined with high complexity.
4. High Variance in Data:
    o Large fluctuations in the data can lead to the model learning noise rather than general patterns.

Strategies to Mitigate Overfitting

1. Regularization:

- L1 Regularization (Lasso): Adds the absolute value of the magnitude of coefficients as a penalty term to the loss function. It encourages sparsity, effectively reducing the number of parameters.
- L2 Regularization (Ridge): Adds the squared magnitude of coefficients as a penalty to the loss function. This discourages large weights and helps in smoothing the model's predictions.
- Dropout: Randomly sets a fraction of the activations in a layer to zero during each training step, preventing the model from becoming overly dependent on specific neurons.

2. Cross-Validation:
   - Use techniques like k-fold cross-validation to evaluate the model's performance on multiple subsets of the data. This helps ensure that the model generalizes well to different portions of the dataset.

3. Early Stopping:
   - Monitor the model's performance on a validation set during training. Stop training when performance on the validation set begins to deteriorate, indicating potential overfitting.

4. Data Augmentation:
   - Apply transformations to the training data (such as rotations, translations, flips, or noise addition) to increase the dataset's size and variability without collecting new data.

5. Simplifying the Model:
   - Reduce the model's complexity by decreasing the number of layers or parameters. A simpler model is less likely to overfit, especially with small datasets.

6. Pruning:
   - Remove unnecessary weights or neurons from the model, making it simpler and less prone to overfitting.

Vanishing Gradients

The vanishing gradient problem occurs during the training of deep neural networks, especially those with many layers. It refers to the scenario where gradients of the loss function with respect to parameters become very small, almost zero, during backpropagation. This causes the weights of the initial layers to update very slowly or not at all, hindering the learning process and resulting in poor performance.

Causes of Vanishing Gradients

1. Activation Functions:
   - Activation functions like the sigmoid or tanh compress inputs to a very small range, especially for large or small input values. This compression leads to very small gradients.
2. Deep Architectures:
   - In very deep networks, the multiplicative effect of chain rule during backpropagation can cause gradients to shrink exponentially as they propagate back through layers.
3. Improper Initialization:
   - Weights initialized too small can exacerbate the vanishing gradient problem by further reducing the magnitude of gradients as they propagate.

Strategies to Address Vanishing Gradients

1. ReLU Activation Function:
   - ReLU (Rectified Linear Unit) activation function outputs zero for negative inputs and

Addressing Challenges: Overfitting and Vanishing Gradients in Training Deep Learning Models

Training deep learning models involves overcoming several challenges to achieve robust and generalizable performance. Two of the most significant challenges are overfitting and vanishing gradients. These issues can severely impact the model's ability to learn effectively and generalize to new data. Understanding these challenges and employing strategies to mitigate them are crucial for developing successful deep learning models.

Overfitting

Overfitting occurs when a model learns the training data too well, capturing not only the underlying patterns but also the noise and outliers. This results in excellent performance on the training data but poor generalization to new, unseen data. Essentially, the model becomes too tailored to the training dataset and fails to perform well on other datasets.

Causes of Overfitting

1. Excessive Model Complexity:
   o Models with too many parameters or excessive depth can capture noise and subtle anomalies in the training data, leading to overfitting.
2. Insufficient Training Data:
   o When there isn't enough data, the model may learn noise and specific details that do not generalize to a broader dataset.

Part IV: AI Applications

Computer Vision

Object Detection and Recognition in Computer Vision

Object detection and recognition are crucial tasks within the field of computer vision, enabling machines to perceive and understand the visual world much like humans do. These processes involve identifying and locating objects within an image or video, classifying them into categories, and sometimes even understanding their relationships.

Object Detection

Object detection refers to the ability to identify and locate objects within an image or video frame. This involves not only recognizing the presence of objects but also determining their positions and sizes, typically by drawing bounding boxes around them.

Key Components of Object Detection

1. Object Localization:
   o Determines the location of objects within the image. This is usually represented by bounding boxes that enclose each detected object.
2. Object Classification:
   o Identifies what the detected object is, assigning it to a category or class from a predefined set (e.g., cat, dog, car).
3. Object Detection:
   o Combines both localization and classification, allowing the system to find and classify multiple objects within the same image.

Common Object Detection Algorithms

1. Region-Based Convolutional Neural Networks (R-CNN):
   o Concept: R-CNN and its variants (Fast R-CNN, Faster R-CNN) first generate region proposals (potential bounding boxes) and then classify these regions to detect objects.
   o Process:
     ▪ Region Proposal: Generate candidate regions that might contain objects.
     ▪ Feature Extraction: Use a CNN to extract features from these regions.
     ▪ Classification: Classify each region using a separate network.

- Applications: Widely used in applications requiring accurate object detection, like autonomous driving and medical imaging.
2. You Only Look Once (YOLO):
   - Concept: YOLO treats object detection as a single regression problem, predicting both bounding boxes and class probabilities directly from full images in one evaluation.
   - Process:
     - Grid Division: Divide the image into a grid.
     - Bounding Box Prediction: Predict bounding boxes and confidence scores for objects within each grid cell.
     - Class Probability Prediction: Assign class probabilities to each bounding box.
   - Advantages: Extremely fast and suitable for real-time applications due to its single-shot detection approach.
   - Applications: Real-time detection in video streams, drone navigation, and robotics.
3. Single Shot Multibox Detector (SSD):
   - Concept: SSD discretizes the output space of bounding boxes into a set of default boxes over different aspect ratios and scales per feature map location.
   - Process:
     - Multi-Scale Feature Maps: Use multiple feature maps at different scales to predict bounding boxes and class scores.
     - Direct Prediction: Predict categories and bounding box offsets for a fixed set of boxes from feature maps.
   - Advantages: Balances accuracy and speed, suitable for mobile and embedded applications.
   - Applications: Object detection on mobile devices and low-latency applications.
4. EfficientDet:
   - Concept: EfficientDet builds on EfficientNet, a family of models that balance accuracy and computational efficiency using a compound scaling method.
   - Process:
     - Feature Pyramid Network (FPN): Integrates features at multiple scales using a bi-directional FPN.
     - Scalable Architecture: Utilizes EfficientNet's backbone for feature extraction, scaled according to the application's needs.
   - Advantages: Provides a good trade-off between speed, size, and accuracy.

o Applications: Ideal for edge devices and applications with constraints on computational resources.

Object Recognition

Object recognition focuses on identifying and classifying objects within images. Unlike object detection, which finds and locates objects, object recognition primarily involves categorizing what is present in the image.

Key Aspects of Object Recognition

1. Image Classification:
   o Assigns a label to an image, identifying the most probable object category that the image belongs to. This does not involve locating the object but rather recognizing its presence.
2. Feature Extraction:
   o Extracts relevant features from images that are then used to identify and classify objects. Features could be edges, textures, colors, or shapes that are distinctive for different classes of objects.
3. Classification Algorithms:
   o Uses algorithms such as Convolutional Neural Networks (CNNs) to process the extracted features and assign a class label to the object.

Common Object Recognition Techniques

1. Convolutional Neural Networks (CNNs):
   o Concept: CNNs are designed to process grid-like data, such as images, by applying convolution operations to extract hierarchical features.
   o Structure:
      ▪ Convolutional Layers: Apply filters to detect features such as edges and textures.
      ▪ Pooling Layers: Reduce the spatial dimensions of the feature maps, preserving important features while reducing computational load.
      ▪ Fully Connected Layers: Use the flattened feature maps to perform classification.
   o Applications: Image classification in fields like healthcare (diagnosing diseases from medical images), retail (product recognition), and security (facial recognition).
2. Transfer Learning:

- ○ Concept: Utilizes pre-trained models on large datasets (like ImageNet) and fine-tunes them on specific tasks with smaller datasets.
- ○ Process:
  - ▪ Pre-trained Model: Start with a model trained on a large, generic dataset.
  - ▪ Fine-Tuning: Adapt the model to the specific task by continuing training on a smaller, task-specific dataset.
- ○ Advantages: Reduces training time and requires less data while leveraging the knowledge from large datasets.
- ○ Applications: Widely used in applications where computational resources or data are limited.
3. Bag of Visual Words (BoVW):
  - ○ Concept: Treats image features like words in a text document, creating a histogram of feature occurrences.
  - ○ Process:
    - ▪ Feature Extraction: Detect key points and extract local features (like SIFT or SURF).

Image Segmentation in Computer Vision

Image segmentation is a critical task in computer vision that involves partitioning an image into meaningful segments, often to simplify or change the representation of an image into something that is more meaningful and easier to analyze. Each segment or region typically represents a different object or part of an object. Unlike object detection, which identifies and locates objects using bounding boxes, segmentation provides a pixel-level understanding of the image.

Types of Image Segmentation

1. Semantic Segmentation:
    - Definition: Assigns a label to each pixel in an image, classifying pixels into categories such as "car," "road," "sky," etc. All pixels belonging to the same category are grouped together without distinguishing between different instances of the same object type.
    - Applications: Autonomous driving (understanding the environment), medical imaging (segmenting anatomical structures), and satellite imagery analysis (land cover classification).
2. Instance Segmentation:
    - Definition: Extends semantic segmentation by identifying each object instance separately. This means distinguishing between individual objects of the same category, such as detecting and labeling each car separately in a traffic scene.
    - Applications: Object counting, scene understanding in robotics, and any task where individual object identification is crucial.
3. Panoptic Segmentation:
    - Definition: Combines both semantic and instance segmentation, providing a unified framework that labels each pixel with both a category and an instance identifier. This approach gives a comprehensive view of the scene, identifying both the type and the specific instance of each object.
    - Applications: Advanced robotics, comprehensive scene understanding, and any application requiring detailed scene analysis.

Techniques and Algorithms for Image Segmentation

1. Classical Methods:

- Thresholding: Converts grayscale images into binary images based on a pixel intensity threshold. It's simple but effective for segmenting images with high contrast between the object and the background.
  - Otsu's Method: An automatic thresholding technique that selects the threshold to minimize the intra-class variance of the segmented regions.
- Edge Detection: Identifies object boundaries by detecting discontinuities in pixel intensity. Techniques like the Canny edge detector are commonly used to outline objects.
- Region-Based Segmentation: Groups pixels into regions based on predefined criteria, such as pixel intensity or texture similarity. Methods include region growing and watershed segmentation.
  - Watershed Algorithm: Treats pixel intensity values as topographic elevations and finds the watershed lines (boundaries) separating different catchment basins (segments).

2. Modern Deep Learning Methods:
- Fully Convolutional Networks (FCNs): Extend traditional CNNs by replacing fully connected layers with convolutional layers to output spatially dense predictions, which are then used for pixel-wise classification.
  - Architecture: Converts input images into lower-dimensional feature maps and then up-samples them to produce dense segmentation maps.
- U-Net: Designed for biomedical image segmentation, it consists of a contracting path to capture context and a symmetric expanding path for precise localization.
  - Architecture: Features a U-shaped structure with a sequence of convolutional and up-sampling layers that provide high-resolution segmentations even with a limited number of training samples.
- Mask R-CNN: Extends Faster R-CNN for object detection by adding a branch for predicting segmentation masks on each region of interest (RoI) in parallel with bounding box recognition and classification.
  - Architecture: Combines RoI Align for accurate localization and a fully convolutional network to predict masks for each detected object.
- DeepLab: A series of architectures that use atrous (dilated) convolutions and spatial pyramid pooling to capture multi-scale context and produce detailed segmentation results.

- DeepLabv3+: Integrates encoder-decoder architecture with atrous separable convolutions for both capturing fine details and understanding context.
3. Graph-Based Methods:
   - Graph Cut: Models the segmentation problem as a graph where pixels are nodes, and edges represent the relationship between them. The segmentation task is solved by finding the minimum cut in the graph.
   - Conditional Random Fields (CRFs): Model the dependencies between neighboring pixels to smooth segmentation maps and refine boundaries.

Applications of Image Segmentation

1. Autonomous Vehicles:
   - Usage: Semantic segmentation helps self-driving cars understand their surroundings by classifying and segmenting road elements, pedestrians, vehicles, and traffic signs, allowing for safer navigation and decision-making.
2. Medical Imaging:
   - Usage: Segmenting different tissues, organs, or abnormalities in medical scans like MRIs or CTs aids in diagnosis, treatment planning, and monitoring. For instance, tumor segmentation in MRI scans is crucial for cancer treatment.
3. Satellite and Aerial Imagery:
   - Usage: Segmentation of satellite images helps in urban planning, agricultural monitoring, and environmental surveillance by classifying land cover types and detecting changes over time.
4. Robotics and Manufacturing:
   - Usage: Enables robots to understand and interact with their environment by segmenting objects for tasks like picking and placing, assembling, and navigating through spaces.
5. Augmented Reality (AR):
   - Usage: Segmenting and understanding the environment allows AR systems to overlay digital content seamlessly on real-world objects, enhancing user experience in gaming, navigation, and training applications.

Natural Language Processing (NLP)

Text Processing and Analysis in Natural Language Processing (NLP)

Natural Language Processing (NLP) is a field of artificial intelligence that focuses on the interaction between computers and human languages. It involves enabling computers to understand, interpret, and respond to human language in a valuable way. Text processing and analysis are fundamental components of NLP, encompassing various techniques and methods to transform raw text into a structured and analyzable format.

Text Processing in NLP

Text processing involves several steps to prepare raw text data for further analysis. These steps are essential for cleaning, transforming, and structuring text so that it can be effectively analyzed and understood by machine learning algorithms.

Key Steps in Text Processing

1. Tokenization:
    o Definition: Tokenization is the process of splitting text into individual units, such as words or sentences, called tokens.
    o Purpose: It simplifies the text into manageable pieces for further processing and analysis.
    o Techniques: Word tokenization (splitting text into words) and sentence tokenization (splitting text into sentences).
    o Example: The sentence "NLP is fascinating!" can be tokenized into ["NLP", "is", "fascinating", "!"].
2. Normalization:
    o Definition: Text normalization involves converting text into a consistent format.
    o Purpose: It ensures uniformity and reduces variations in text data that could affect analysis.
    o Techniques:
        ▪ Lowercasing: Converts all characters in the text to lowercase.
        ▪ Removing Punctuation: Strips punctuation marks from the text.
        ▪ Removing Stop Words: Eliminates common but uninformative words (e.g., "and," "the," "is").
        ▪ Example: Normalizing "The QUICK brown fox!" results in "the quick brown fox."

3. Stemming and Lemmatization:
   o Stemming:
     ▪ Definition: Reduces words to their root form by removing suffixes.
     ▪ Purpose: Simplifies variations of a word to a common base form.
     ▪ Example: "Running," "runner," and "ran" can be stemmed to "run."
   o Lemmatization:
     ▪ Definition: Reduces words to their base or dictionary form, known as a lemma.
     ▪ Purpose: Provides a more accurate reduction than stemming by considering the context and morphological analysis.
     ▪ Example: "Better" lemmatizes to "good," considering the context of comparative form.
4. Part-of-Speech (POS) Tagging:
   o Definition: POS tagging assigns grammatical tags to each word in a sentence, indicating its role (e.g., noun, verb, adjective).
   o Purpose: Helps in understanding the syntactic structure and context of the text.
   o Example: In the sentence "The quick brown fox jumps," "The" is a determiner, "quick" and "brown" are adjectives, "fox" is a noun, and "jumps" is a verb.
5. Named Entity Recognition (NER):
   o Definition: NER identifies and classifies entities within text into predefined categories such as names, dates, organizations, and locations.
   o Purpose: Extracts meaningful information and facilitates tasks like information retrieval and knowledge extraction.
   o Example: In the sentence "Google was founded in September 1998 by Larry Page and Sergey Brin," NER identifies "Google" as an organization, "September 1998" as a date, and "Larry Page" and "Sergey Brin" as persons.
6. Syntactic Parsing:
   o Definition: Syntactic parsing involves analyzing the grammatical structure of a sentence to understand the relationships between words.
   o Purpose: Provides a tree structure representation that illustrates the syntactic organization of the text.
   o Techniques: Dependency parsing and constituency parsing.

- o Example: Parsing the sentence "The quick brown fox jumps over the lazy dog" identifies the subject ("fox"), verb ("jumps"), and object ("dog").
7. Text Vectorization:
   - o Definition: Converts text into numerical representations that machine learning models can process.
   - o Purpose: Enables text data to be used in algorithms that require numerical input.
   - o Techniques:
     - Bag of Words (BoW): Represents text as a set of word frequencies, disregarding grammar and word order.
     - Term Frequency-Inverse Document Frequency (TF-IDF): Weighs word importance based on its frequency in the document relative to its frequency across all documents.
     - Word Embeddings: Maps words to dense vector spaces capturing semantic relationships (e.g., Word2Vec, GloVe, FastText).
   - o Example: The word "king" might be represented as a vector [0.25, -0.75, ...] in an embedding space.

Text Analysis in NLP

Text analysis builds on processed text to extract meaningful insights, discover patterns, and understand context. It involves various analytical techniques to derive semantic information from text data.

Key Techniques in Text Analysis

1. Sentiment Analysis:
   - o Definition: Sentiment analysis determines the sentiment or emotion expressed in a piece of text, categorizing it as positive, negative, or neutral.
   - o Purpose: Useful for understanding public opinion, customer feedback, and social media monitoring.
   - o Techniques: Rule-based methods, machine learning models, and deep learning approaches.
   - o Example: Analyzing a review "The product is amazing and very affordable!" would classify it as positive sentiment.
2. Topic Modeling:

- o Definition: Topic modeling uncovers hidden topics or themes within a large collection of documents.
- o Purpose: Helps in organizing and summarizing large text corpora.
- o Techniques:
  - Latent Dirichlet Allocation (LDA): Assumes documents are mixtures of topics and topics are mixtures of words, inferring the distribution of topics in documents.
  - Non-Negative Matrix Factorization (NMF): Decomposes the document-term matrix into lower-dimensional matrices to identify latent topics.
- o Example: In a set of news articles, topic modeling might reveal topics like "politics," "sports," and "technology."

3. Text Classification:
   - o Definition: Text classification assigns predefined labels to text based on its content.
   - o Purpose: Used in spam detection, sentiment classification, and categorizing news articles.
   - o Techniques: Naive Bayes, Support Vector Machines, and neural networks.
   - o Example: Classifying emails as "spam" or "not spam."

4. Named Entity Recognition (NER):
   - o Definition: Identifies and classifies entities in text into categories such as names, dates, organizations, and locations.
   - o Purpose: Facilitates the extraction of structured information from unstructured text.
   - o Techniques: Machine learning models and rule-based approaches.
   - o Example: Extracting entities like "New York" (location) and "Apple Inc." (organization) from a news article.

5. Summarization:
   - o Definition: Summarization condenses a document to its key points and main ideas, producing a shorter version.
   - o Purpose: Provides quick insights into large volumes of text and facilitates easier information consumption.
   - o Techniques:
     - Extractive Summarization: Selects key sentences or phrases directly from the text to create a summary.
     - Abstractive Summarization: Generates a summary by interpreting and rephrasing the original text in a concise form.
   - o Example: Summarizing a lengthy research paper to highlight the main findings and conclusions.

6. Machine Translation:
   - Definition: Translates text from one language to another using computational algorithms.
   - Purpose: Enables cross-lingual communication and accessibility of information.
   - Techniques: Rule-based systems, statistical machine translation, and neural machine translation (e.g., Seq2Seq models, Transformer models).
   - Example: Translating an English sentence "How are you?" to Spanish "¿Cómo estás?".

Language Models and Transformers in Natural Language Processing (NLP)

In the domain of Natural Language Processing (NLP), language models and transformers represent significant advancements that have revolutionized how machines understand and generate human language. These models leverage deep learning techniques to capture the nuances and complexities of language, enabling a wide range of applications from text generation to translation and beyond.

Language Models

Language models are algorithms that can predict the next word in a sequence given the preceding words. They form the backbone of many NLP applications by understanding the probability distribution of sequences of words. These models can be broadly categorized into statistical and neural language models.

1. Statistical Language Models:

    o Definition: These models use statistical techniques to calculate the likelihood of word sequences based on observed frequency data.

    o Types:

        ▪ n-gram Models: Predict the next word in a sequence based on the preceding n-1 words. They are simple but often struggle with longer dependencies due to limited context windows.

            ▪ Example: A bigram model (n=2) would predict the next word based on the previous one, e.g., "The cat" might predict "sat" with a higher probability than "runs".

        ▪ Hidden Markov Models (HMMs): Use probabilistic methods to model sequences and their transitions, often applied in tasks like part-of-speech tagging and speech recognition.

2. Neural Language Models:

    o Definition: These models use neural networks to learn the complex patterns and relationships in language from large datasets. They can capture more context and subtle nuances compared to statistical models.

- o Types:

    - Recurrent Neural Networks (RNNs): Designed to handle sequential data by maintaining a memory of previous inputs, allowing them to model long-term dependencies.

        - LSTM and GRU: Variants of RNNs that solve the problem of vanishing gradients, making them effective for capturing long-range dependencies in sequences.

    - Transformers: Advanced neural architectures that use self-attention mechanisms to handle long-range dependencies more efficiently than RNNs.

        - Self-Attention: Allows the model to weigh the importance of different words in a sequence when making predictions, regardless of their position in the sequence.

Transformers

Transformers represent a breakthrough in NLP due to their ability to process and understand sequences of text without relying on sequential data processing. This innovation allows for parallel processing of data, leading to significant improvements in efficiency and scalability.

1. Architecture:

    - o Components:

        - Encoder: Processes the input sequence and creates a representation (embedding) for each word in the context of the sequence.

        - Decoder: Generates the output sequence from the embeddings created by the encoder. In many transformer models used for language understanding, the decoder is not used.

- Self-Attention Mechanism: Evaluates the relationship between all words in the input sequence to understand the context more comprehensively.

- Positional Encoding: Adds information about the position of words in the sequence, addressing the fact that transformers process all words simultaneously without an inherent notion of order.

2. Key Transformer Models:

   o BERT (Bidirectional Encoder Representations from Transformers):

   - Overview: BERT is designed to pre-train deep bidirectional representations by jointly conditioning on both left and right context in all layers.

   - Training:

     - Masked Language Modeling (MLM): Randomly masks some words in the input sequence and trains the model to predict them based on their context.

     - Next Sentence Prediction (NSP): Trains the model to understand sentence relationships by predicting if a given sentence follows another.

   - Applications: BERT is fine-tuned for various tasks like question answering, sentiment analysis, and text classification.

   - Strengths: Its bidirectional approach captures more context and dependencies than unidirectional models.

   - Example: In the sentence pair "The cat sat on the mat. It looked very comfortable.", BERT can use context from both sentences to understand that "It" refers to "The cat".

   o GPT (Generative Pre-trained Transformer):

- Overview: GPT focuses on language generation and unidirectional context, predicting the next word in a sequence based on the preceding words.

- Training:

  - Causal Language Modeling (CLM): Trains the model to predict the next word in a sequence, using only the left context.

- Applications: GPT excels in text generation tasks, conversational agents, and creating coherent and contextually appropriate continuations of text.

- Strengths: Its generative capabilities make it highly effective for tasks requiring the generation of fluent and coherent text.

- Example: Given the prompt "Once upon a time in a land far away,", GPT can generate a continuation like "there lived a wise old owl who knew the secrets of the forest."

o T5 (Text-to-Text Transfer Transformer):

  - Overview: T5 frames all NLP tasks as a text-to-text problem, where both the input and output are text sequences.

  - Training:

    - Unified Framework: Uses a single model to handle diverse tasks by converting them into text generation problems.

  - Applications: T5 can be applied to translation, summarization, and question answering, all within the same model architecture.

  - Strengths: Its unified approach simplifies training and fine-tuning across different tasks.

- Example: For a translation task, given the input "translate English to French: How are you?", T5 can generate "Comment ça va ?".

  ○ RoBERTa (Robustly Optimized BERT Approach):

  - Overview: An optimized version of BERT that achieves improved performance through extended training, larger batch sizes, and more training data.

  - Training:

    - Enhanced Pre-training: Removes the NSP objective and increases training data and steps.

  - Applications: Like BERT, it's used for a wide range of language understanding tasks but with improved robustness and accuracy.

  - Strengths: Better pre-training techniques lead to superior performance on downstream tasks.

  - Example: On a sentiment analysis task, given the input "The movie was absolutely

Real-World Applications of NLP: Chatbots, Translation, and Sentiment Analysis

Natural Language Processing (NLP) has revolutionized the way machines interact with human language, leading to numerous practical applications that impact daily life and business operations. Three prominent applications are chatbots, translation, and sentiment analysis. Each of these leverages the power of NLP to provide intelligent, context-aware, and efficient solutions.

1. Chatbots

Chatbots are AI-powered systems designed to simulate human conversation. They use NLP techniques to understand and respond to user queries, providing automated assistance across various platforms like websites, mobile apps, and social media.

Key Features and Functions:

- Understanding User Intent: Chatbots analyze the input text to determine the user's intent. This involves recognizing the context and purpose behind the user's message.
- Natural Language Understanding (NLU): Enables chatbots to parse and comprehend the user's language, including slang, idioms, and variations in phrasing.
- Dialogue Management: Manages the flow of conversation, ensuring coherent and contextually appropriate responses.
- Response Generation: Uses predefined templates or generates responses dynamically based on the context and intent identified.

Technologies:

- Rule-Based Chatbots: Follow predefined scripts and respond to specific inputs based on set rules. They are straightforward but limited in handling complex or varied queries.
- AI-Powered Chatbots: Use machine learning models, particularly deep learning, to understand and generate responses. They can learn from interactions and improve over time.
- Transformers: Advanced models like BERT and GPT are used to enhance understanding and generate more human-like responses in chatbots.

Applications:

- Customer Service: Companies use chatbots to provide instant support, answer frequently asked questions, and guide users through troubleshooting processes.
- E-commerce: Chatbots assist customers with product recommendations, order tracking, and making purchases.
- Healthcare: Virtual assistants help patients schedule appointments, provide medical information, and remind them to take medications.
- Banking: Chatbots facilitate banking operations like checking account balances, transferring money, and providing financial advice.

Example:

- Customer Support Bot: A telecom company's chatbot can handle queries like "How do I reset my password?" or "What's my current bill amount?" by providing quick, accurate answers or guiding the user through the steps.

2. Translation

Translation involves converting text or speech from one language to another. NLP-powered translation systems aim to preserve the meaning, tone, and context of the original language in the target language.

Key Features and Functions:

- Language Pair Support: Supports translation between multiple languages, from widely spoken ones like English and Spanish to less common languages.
- Context Preservation: Ensures that translated content maintains the context and intent of the original text, not just the literal word meanings.
- Idiomatic Expressions: Accurately translates phrases and idioms that might not have direct equivalents in the target language.
- Voice Translation: Converts spoken language in real-time, facilitating multilingual conversations.

Technologies:

- Statistical Machine Translation (SMT): Uses statistical models to generate translations based on the analysis of bilingual text corpora.

- Neural Machine Translation (NMT): Employs deep learning models to produce more fluent and accurate translations by understanding the context of entire sentences.
- Transformers: Models like the Transformer architecture, BERT, and GPT, which capture long-range dependencies and context, significantly enhance the quality of machine translation.

Applications:

- Global Communication: Facilitates communication between speakers of different languages in international business, diplomacy, and social interactions.
- Content Localization: Translates websites, software, and multimedia content for global audiences, ensuring cultural and linguistic appropriateness.
- Travel and Tourism: Mobile apps and devices provide real-time translation services for travelers navigating foreign languages.
- Education: Helps students and professionals access educational materials and research in different languages.

Example:

- Google Translate: A widely used translation service that supports text, speech, and image translation across numerous languages, leveraging NMT for improved accuracy and fluency.

3. Sentiment Analysis

Sentiment analysis, also known as opinion mining, involves determining the emotional tone behind a body of text. It categorizes opinions expressed in text as positive, negative, or neutral, and can also detect more nuanced sentiments like joy, anger, or surprise.

Key Features and Functions:

- Polarity Detection: Classifies text into categories based on sentiment polarity (positive, negative, neutral).
- Emotion Detection: Identifies specific emotions expressed in the text, such as happiness, sadness, anger, or excitement.
- Aspect-Based Sentiment Analysis: Analyzes sentiments related to specific aspects or features within the text (e.g., product reviews).

- Trend Analysis: Tracks sentiment trends over time, useful for monitoring public opinion or customer satisfaction.

Technologies:

- Lexicon-Based Approaches: Use predefined lists of words associated with specific sentiments to evaluate text.
- Machine Learning Models: Train classifiers (e.g., Support Vector Machines, Logistic Regression) on labeled datasets to predict sentiment based on features extracted from text.
- Deep Learning: Neural networks, including RNNs and transformers like BERT, are used for more accurate sentiment analysis by capturing context and subtleties in language.

Applications:

- Customer Feedback Analysis: Businesses analyze reviews and feedback to gauge customer satisfaction and identify areas for improvement.
- Social Media Monitoring: Organizations track sentiment trends and public opinion on social platforms to understand brand perception and respond to issues.
- Market Research: Companies analyze consumer sentiments toward products or services to inform marketing strategies and product development.
- Political Analysis: Researchers and analysts evaluate public opinion on policies, events, and political figures through sentiment analysis of social media and news content.

Example:

- Twitter Sentiment Analysis: Tools analyze tweets to determine public sentiment about a new product launch, political event, or social issue, helping organizations understand public reactions in real-time.

Robotics and Autonomous Systems

Basics of Robotics

Robotics is a multidisciplinary field involving the design, construction, operation, and use of robots. Robots are autonomous or semi-autonomous systems capable of performing tasks in various environments, often mimicking human actions or operating in areas where human intervention is impractical or hazardous. The field encompasses aspects of engineering, computer science, artificial intelligence, and more, aiming to develop machines that can assist, augment, or replace human efforts in various tasks.

Core Components of Robotics

To understand the basics of robotics, it's essential to grasp its core components, each contributing to a robot's functionality and versatility:

1. Mechanical Structure:

    o Definition: The physical framework of a robot, often composed of a body, limbs, and actuators.

    o Components:

        ▪ Chassis/Frame: The base structure that supports all other components.

        ▪ Actuators: Motors or other mechanisms that produce movement. Common types include electric motors, hydraulic systems, and pneumatic systems.

        ▪ End Effectors: Tools or devices attached to the robot's limbs to interact with the environment (e.g., grippers, welders, sensors).

    o Purpose: Provides the structural integrity and movement capabilities, enabling the robot to perform tasks like walking, grasping, or manipulating objects.

2. Sensors:

    o Definition: Devices that gather data from the environment and the robot's own state.

- Types:

  - Vision Sensors: Cameras and optical sensors for image and video capture.

  - Touch Sensors: Detect physical contact or pressure (tactile sensors).

  - Proximity Sensors: Measure the distance to nearby objects (e.g., infrared, ultrasonic).

  - Gyroscopes and Accelerometers: Monitor orientation, balance, and movement.

- Purpose: Enable the robot to perceive its surroundings and make informed decisions based on real-time data.

3. Control Systems:

   - Definition: Software and algorithms that govern the robot's actions and responses.

   - Components:

     - Microcontrollers: Small, programmable computers that control specific tasks.

     - Central Processing Units (CPUs): Handle complex computations and coordinate multiple tasks.

     - Firmware: Embedded software that manages the hardware functions.

   - Purpose: Processes sensor inputs, executes programmed instructions, and sends commands to actuators, ensuring the robot behaves as intended.

4. Power Supply:

   - Definition: Provides the energy required to operate the robot.

   - Types:

- Batteries: Common in mobile robots, providing portable energy.

- Direct Power: Connected to an external power source, typical for stationary robots.

- Solar Cells: Used in robots designed for outdoor or long-term applications.

  o Purpose: Powers the robot's motors, sensors, and control systems.

5. Communication Systems:

  o Definition: Enable data exchange between the robot and other systems or operators.

  o Types:

    - Wired Communication: Direct connections using cables.

    - Wireless Communication: Technologies like Wi-Fi, Bluetooth, or cellular networks.

  o Purpose: Facilitates remote control, monitoring, and data sharing.

Types of Robots

Robots are classified based on their application, form, and autonomy. Here are some common categories:

1. Industrial Robots:

  o Description: Used in manufacturing and production environments for tasks such as assembly, welding, painting, and material handling.

  o Characteristics: Typically stationary, high precision, and often operate in predefined patterns.

  o Examples: Robotic arms used in car assembly lines.

2. Service Robots:

- o Description: Assist humans in non-industrial environments, providing services ranging from personal assistance to entertainment.

- o Characteristics: Can be mobile or stationary, and are often designed for direct interaction with humans.

- o Examples: Home cleaning robots like Roomba, robotic waiters.

3. Medical Robots:

- o Description: Specialized for healthcare applications, such as surgery, rehabilitation, and patient care.

- o Characteristics: Require high precision and reliability, often with advanced sensing and control capabilities.

- o Examples: Surgical robots like the Da Vinci system, robotic prosthetics.

4. Exploration Robots:

- o Description: Operate in remote or hazardous environments to gather data and perform tasks.

- o Characteristics: Designed to withstand extreme conditions, often autonomous or remotely controlled.

- o Examples: Mars rovers like Curiosity, underwater exploration robots.

5. Humanoid Robots:

- o Description: Designed to resemble and mimic human form and movements.

- o Characteristics: Bipedal locomotion, human-like interaction capabilities.

- o Examples: ASIMO by Honda, Atlas by Boston Dynamics.

6. Autonomous Vehicles:

- o Description: Self-driving vehicles capable of navigating and operating without human intervention.

- o Characteristics: Utilize advanced sensors, mapping, and AI to drive safely and efficiently.

- o Examples: Autonomous cars, drones.

Key Concepts in Robotics

1. Autonomy Levels:

    - o Manual: Operated entirely by human control.

    - o Semi-Autonomous: Perform tasks with some degree of human oversight.

    - o Fully Autonomous: Operate independently without human intervention, often using AI and machine learning.

2. Kinematics and Dynamics:

    - o Kinematics: Study of motion without considering forces. Involves the geometry and movement of robot parts.

    - o Dynamics: Study of forces and torques and their effect on motion. Crucial for controlling movement and maintaining stability.

3. Control Theory:

    - o Definition: Mathematical framework for designing systems that control the behavior of robots to achieve desired outputs.

    - o Applications: Used in trajectory planning, stability maintenance, and responsive behavior.

4. Path Planning and Navigation:

    - o Path Planning: Algorithms that determine the optimal path for a robot to reach a destination.

- Navigation: Techniques that enable a robot to move through its environment, avoiding obstacles and adjusting to changes.

5. Artificial Intelligence (AI) in Robotics:

   - Role: Enhances the decision-making capabilities of robots, enabling them to learn from experiences and adapt to new situations.

   - Techniques: Machine learning, computer vision, and natural language processing are often integrated into robotic systems.

Integration of AI in Robotics

The integration of Artificial Intelligence (AI) in robotics is revolutionizing the capabilities and applications of robotic systems. By combining AI with robotics, we enhance robots' ability to perform complex tasks, adapt to dynamic environments, and improve efficiency and accuracy in various applications. Here's a detailed look at how AI integrates with robotics and its significance.

Key Areas of AI Integration in Robotics

1. Perception and Sensing:

    o Computer Vision: AI algorithms, particularly deep learning models, process and interpret visual data from cameras and sensors. This enables robots to recognize objects, understand scenes, and navigate environments.

        ▪ Example: Autonomous vehicles use computer vision to detect pedestrians, other vehicles, and traffic signals.

    o Sensor Fusion: Combining data from multiple sensors (e.g., cameras, LiDAR, ultrasonic sensors) to create a comprehensive understanding of the robot's surroundings.

        ▪ Example: Robots in manufacturing use sensor fusion to monitor product quality and detect defects in real-time.

2. Decision Making and Planning:

    o Path Planning: AI algorithms compute optimal paths for robots to follow, considering obstacles and dynamic changes in the environment.

        ▪ Example: Delivery robots use AI-based path planning to navigate crowded urban areas efficiently.

    o Autonomous Navigation: Robots use AI to navigate and perform tasks without human intervention, relying on real-time data and pre-learned models.

- Example: Drones use AI to autonomously survey agricultural fields, collect data, and avoid obstacles.

3. Learning and Adaptation:

   o Machine Learning: Robots are equipped with machine learning models that allow them to learn from experience and improve their performance over time.

      - Example: Service robots in hospitality learn from interactions with guests to provide better and more personalized services.

   o Reinforcement Learning: Robots learn optimal behaviors through trial and error, receiving feedback from their environment to refine their actions.

      - Example: Robots in warehouses use reinforcement learning to optimize picking and placing tasks, reducing time and errors.

4. Human-Robot Interaction:

   o Natural Language Processing (NLP): AI enables robots to understand and respond to human language, facilitating more natural and intuitive interactions.

      - Example: Customer service robots use NLP to understand customer queries and provide relevant responses.

   o Emotion Recognition: AI algorithms analyze human facial expressions and vocal tones to gauge emotions, enabling robots to respond appropriately.

      - Example: Companion robots for elderly care use emotion recognition to provide comfort and support based on the user's emotional state.

5. Robotic Control:

- o Adaptive Control Systems: AI enhances traditional control systems by allowing robots to adapt to changing conditions and uncertainties in real-time.

    - Example: Industrial robots use adaptive control to adjust their operations based on variations in assembly line conditions.

- o Predictive Maintenance: AI models predict when a robot might fail or require maintenance, preventing downtime and extending the robot's operational life.

    - Example: Factory robots are monitored using AI to predict wear and tear, scheduling maintenance before a breakdown occurs.

Significance of AI in Robotics

1. Enhanced Autonomy: AI allows robots to operate independently without constant human supervision, increasing efficiency and reducing operational costs.

    - o Example: Autonomous cleaning robots in commercial buildings can clean floors, avoid obstacles, and recharge themselves without human intervention.

2. Improved Efficiency and Accuracy: AI-driven robots perform tasks with higher precision and speed, leading to increased productivity and consistency in various industries.

    - o Example: In agriculture, AI-powered robots can accurately identify and harvest ripe fruits, reducing waste and increasing yield.

3. Adaptability to Dynamic Environments: AI enables robots to adapt to unpredictable and changing environments, making them suitable for a broader range of applications.

    - o Example: Search and rescue robots use AI to navigate through rubble and locate survivors in disaster-stricken areas.

4. Enhanced Safety: AI enhances the safety of robotic operations by enabling robots to detect and respond to hazards, ensuring safe interaction with humans and other machines.

   o Example: Collaborative robots (cobots) in manufacturing can work alongside humans, stopping immediately if they detect any potential danger.

5. Personalization: AI allows robots to provide personalized experiences by learning individual preferences and behaviors.

   o Example: Personal assistant robots learn a user's daily routine and preferences, offering tailored assistance and reminders.

Real-World Applications

1. Healthcare: AI-powered robots assist in surgeries, patient care, and rehabilitation, improving outcomes and efficiency.

   o Example: Surgical robots perform minimally invasive surgeries with precision guided by AI algorithms.

2. Manufacturing: AI enhances automation in manufacturing, from assembly lines to quality control.

   o Example: AI-driven robotic arms assemble electronic components with high accuracy, reducing defects and increasing production rates.

3. Logistics: AI optimizes logistics operations, including warehouse management and delivery.

   o Example: Automated guided vehicles (AGVs) in warehouses use AI to optimize routes and manage inventory.

4. Entertainment: AI-integrated robots provide interactive and engaging experiences in entertainment and education.

   o Example: Robots in theme parks interact with visitors, providing information and entertainment through AI-powered interactions.

Applications of AI in Robotics: Industrial Robots, Drones, Autonomous Vehicles

The integration of Artificial Intelligence (AI) in robotics has significantly advanced the capabilities of various types of robots, leading to their widespread application across multiple domains. Three notable applications include industrial robots, drones, and autonomous vehicles. Each of these utilizes AI to perform tasks more efficiently, accurately, and autonomously.

1. Industrial Robots

Industrial robots are automated machines used in manufacturing and production environments to perform repetitive or dangerous tasks with high precision and efficiency.

Key Applications:

- Assembly Line Automation: Robots assemble parts with precision, enhancing production speed and consistency.
    - Example: Automotive manufacturers use robotic arms to assemble car components, ensuring high quality and reducing human error.
- Welding and Painting: Robots perform welding and painting tasks with uniformity and safety, protecting workers from hazardous conditions.
    - Example: Robotic welders in metal fabrication create strong, consistent welds, while painting robots ensure an even coat without exposure to toxic fumes.
- Material Handling: Robots transport materials and products within factories, streamlining logistics and reducing manual labor.
    - Example: Automated Guided Vehicles (AGVs) move parts between workstations, optimizing workflow and reducing delays.
- Quality Control: AI-powered vision systems inspect products for defects, ensuring high standards and reducing waste.
    - Example: Camera-equipped robots scan and analyze products for imperfections, automatically sorting out defective items.

Benefits:

- Increased Productivity: Robots operate continuously without fatigue, significantly boosting production rates.

- Enhanced Precision: High accuracy reduces errors and waste, improving product quality.
- Improved Safety: Robots perform hazardous tasks, protecting human workers from dangerous environments.

2. Drones

Drones, or Unmanned Aerial Vehicles (UAVs), are aircraft that operate without a human pilot on board. They are used in a variety of applications, leveraging AI to navigate and perform tasks autonomously.

Key Applications:

- Aerial Surveillance and Monitoring: Drones equipped with cameras and sensors monitor large areas, providing real-time data and surveillance.
  - Example: Agricultural drones survey crops, monitor plant health, and optimize resource usage by analyzing aerial imagery.
- Delivery Services: AI-powered drones deliver packages quickly and efficiently, especially in hard-to-reach areas.
  - Example: Companies like Amazon use delivery drones to transport small packages directly to customers' doorsteps, reducing delivery times.
- Disaster Response and Search & Rescue: Drones assist in emergency situations, locating survivors and assessing damage in disaster-stricken areas.
  - Example: During natural disasters, drones survey affected areas, identify trapped individuals, and deliver essential supplies.
- Inspection and Maintenance: Drones inspect infrastructure such as bridges, power lines, and wind turbines, identifying issues without requiring human access.
  - Example: Energy companies use drones to inspect solar panels and wind turbines, detecting faults and optimizing maintenance schedules.

Benefits:

- Accessibility: Drones reach remote or hazardous locations that are difficult or dangerous for humans.
- Efficiency: Drones perform tasks quickly and can cover large areas in a short time.

- Cost-Effectiveness: Reduces the need for expensive manned aircraft or extensive manual labor.

3. Autonomous Vehicles

Autonomous vehicles are self-driving cars, trucks, and other transportation systems that operate without human intervention. They utilize AI to navigate, make decisions, and interact with their environment.

Key Applications:

- Passenger Transport: Self-driving cars offer a safer and more efficient mode of transport by reducing human error and optimizing routes.
  - Example: Companies like Waymo and Tesla develop autonomous cars that navigate city streets and highways, providing a driverless transportation option.
- Freight and Logistics: Autonomous trucks and delivery vehicles streamline logistics by transporting goods efficiently across long distances.
  - Example: Autonomous trucks by companies like TuSimple transport cargo between distribution centers, reducing reliance on human drivers and cutting transportation costs.
- Public Transportation: Autonomous buses and shuttles provide efficient and accessible public transport options, reducing traffic congestion and emissions.
  - Example: Autonomous shuttles operate in smart cities, offering convenient and environmentally friendly public transportation.
- Ride-Sharing: Autonomous ride-sharing services offer on-demand transportation without the need for human drivers.
  - Example: Companies like Uber and Lyft explore autonomous vehicles for their ride-sharing fleets, enhancing service availability and reducing costs.

Benefits:

- Safety: AI reduces accidents by minimizing human error and adhering strictly to traffic laws.
- Efficiency: Autonomous vehicles optimize routes, reduce traffic congestion, and improve fuel efficiency.
- Accessibility: Provides mobility solutions for individuals unable to drive, such as the elderly or disabled.

AI in Healthcare

Diagnostic systems

AI in Healthcare: Diagnostic Systems

Artificial Intelligence (AI) is revolutionizing the healthcare industry, particularly in the realm of diagnostic systems. AI-driven diagnostic tools leverage advanced algorithms and machine learning to analyze medical data, aiding in the accurate and timely diagnosis of diseases. This transformation in diagnostics promises to enhance patient outcomes, streamline clinical workflows, and reduce healthcare costs.

Key Components of AI Diagnostic Systems

1. Data Collection and Integration:

   - Electronic Health Records (EHRs): Aggregating patient data from various sources, including medical history, laboratory results, imaging, and genetic information.

   - Medical Imaging: Utilizing data from X-rays, MRI, CT scans, and other imaging modalities.

   - Wearable Devices: Collecting continuous health data through smartwatches, fitness trackers, and medical devices.

2. Machine Learning Algorithms:

   - Supervised Learning: Training models on labeled datasets to recognize patterns and make predictions.

   - Deep Learning: Utilizing neural networks, especially convolutional neural networks (CNNs), for image recognition and natural language processing tasks.

   - Natural Language Processing (NLP): Analyzing textual data from medical records and literature to extract relevant information.

3. Predictive Analytics:

   - Risk Stratification: Identifying patients at high risk of developing specific conditions.

- Outcome Prediction: Forecasting disease progression and potential complications.

Applications of AI in Diagnostic Systems

1. Medical Imaging Analysis:

    - Radiology: AI algorithms analyze radiographic images to detect abnormalities such as tumors, fractures, and infections.

        - Example: AI-powered tools can highlight areas of concern in mammograms, assisting radiologists in the early detection of breast cancer.

    - Pathology: AI systems analyze histopathological slides to identify cancerous cells and other anomalies.

        - Example: Deep learning models can classify skin lesions with a high degree of accuracy, aiding dermatologists in diagnosing skin cancers.

2. Genomic Data Analysis:

    - Genetic Screening: AI tools analyze genetic sequences to identify mutations associated with hereditary diseases.

        - Example: AI platforms can predict the likelihood of developing conditions like cystic fibrosis or BRCA-related breast cancer by analyzing genetic markers.

    - Personalized Medicine: Tailoring treatments based on an individual's genetic profile.

        - Example: AI-driven analysis helps in identifying the most effective cancer treatments based on the genetic makeup of a tumor.

3. Predictive Diagnostics:

    - Early Detection: AI systems predict the onset of diseases by analyzing patterns in patient data.

- Example: Machine learning models can predict the development of diabetes or cardiovascular diseases based on lifestyle and biometric data.

  o Chronic Disease Management: Monitoring and managing chronic conditions by predicting flare-ups or complications.

- Example: AI tools help manage chronic obstructive pulmonary disease (COPD) by predicting exacerbations and recommending interventions.

4. Decision Support Systems:

  o Clinical Decision Support: Providing clinicians with evidence-based recommendations and diagnostic suggestions.

- Example: AI systems assist doctors in diagnosing complex cases by cross-referencing symptoms with vast medical databases.

  o Workflow Optimization: Streamlining diagnostic processes and reducing the burden on healthcare providers.

- Example: AI triage systems prioritize cases based on severity, ensuring timely attention to critical patients.

Benefits of AI in Diagnostic Systems

1. Improved Accuracy:

  o Enhanced Precision: AI algorithms often exceed human accuracy in diagnosing conditions from medical images and data.

  o Reduced Error Rates: Minimizing misdiagnosis and missed diagnoses by providing consistent and thorough analysis.

2. Early Detection:

  o Proactive Healthcare: Identifying diseases at earlier stages when they are more treatable.

- o Better Prognosis: Improving patient outcomes through timely intervention.

3. Increased Efficiency:

- o Faster Diagnosis: Accelerating the diagnostic process, enabling quicker decision-making and treatment.

- o Resource Optimization: Reducing the workload on healthcare professionals and allowing them to focus on more complex cases.

4. Personalized Medicine:

- o Tailored Treatments: Customizing treatment plans based on individual patient data, leading to better efficacy.

- o Patient-Specific Insights: Providing insights that are specific to a patient's genetic and health profile.

5. Cost Reduction:

- o Lower Healthcare Costs: Decreasing the need for unnecessary tests and procedures through accurate and early diagnosis.

- o Efficient Resource Use: Optimizing the use of medical resources and reducing hospital stays.

Challenges and Considerations

1. Data Privacy and Security:

- o Protecting Patient Information: Ensuring that patient data is securely stored and transmitted to prevent breaches.

- o Compliance with Regulations: Adhering to healthcare regulations such as HIPAA in the U.S.

2. Bias and Fairness:

- o Algorithmic Bias: Addressing biases in AI models that may lead to disparities in diagnosis and treatment.

- o Inclusive Datasets: Ensuring that training datasets are diverse and representative of different populations.

3. Integration with Clinical Workflows:

   - o User Acceptance: Gaining trust and acceptance from healthcare providers to use AI tools in their practice.

   - o Interoperability: Ensuring that AI systems seamlessly integrate with existing healthcare IT systems.

AI in Healthcare: Personalized Medicine

Personalized medicine, also known as precision medicine, is an innovative approach to healthcare that tailors medical treatment to the individual characteristics of each patient. This approach considers genetic, environmental, and lifestyle factors to develop customized treatment plans. AI plays a critical role in advancing personalized medicine by analyzing vast amounts of data to identify patterns and make predictions that guide individualized treatment strategies.

Key Components of AI in Personalized Medicine

1. Genomic Analysis:

    o Genetic Sequencing: AI algorithms analyze genetic data to identify mutations and variations that influence disease risk and drug response.

        ▪ Example: AI tools can identify genetic markers associated with diseases such as cancer, enabling early detection and targeted therapies.

    o Pharmacogenomics: AI helps in understanding how genetic variations affect individual responses to medications, allowing for more effective and safer drug prescriptions.

        ▪ Example: An AI system can predict how a patient will metabolize certain drugs, helping doctors choose the most effective treatment with minimal side effects.

2. Data Integration and Analysis:

    o Electronic Health Records (EHRs): AI integrates and analyzes data from EHRs, including medical history, laboratory results, and imaging studies, to provide a comprehensive understanding of a patient's health.

        ▪ Example: AI systems can identify patterns in patient data that correlate with disease progression or treatment outcomes.

- ○ Wearable Devices: AI processes continuous health data from wearable devices to monitor patient health in real-time and provide personalized recommendations.

  - ▪ Example: Wearable devices track vital signs and activity levels, with AI analyzing this data to offer insights into lifestyle changes that can improve health outcomes.

3. Predictive Modeling:

  - ○ Risk Prediction: AI models predict an individual's risk of developing specific diseases based on genetic and environmental factors.

    - ▪ Example: AI can assess a person's risk of heart disease by analyzing genetic data, lifestyle factors, and family history.

  - ○ Outcome Prediction: AI predicts how a patient is likely to respond to different treatments, helping doctors choose the most effective therapy.

    - ▪ Example: Predictive models can forecast the effectiveness of cancer treatments based on the molecular profile of a tumor.

Applications of AI in Personalized Medicine

1. Targeted Therapies:

  - ○ Cancer Treatment: AI-driven precision oncology identifies specific genetic mutations in tumors, allowing for targeted therapies that attack cancer cells without harming healthy tissue.

    - ▪ Example: AI can match patients with the most effective cancer treatments based on the genetic characteristics of their tumor.

  - ○ Chronic Disease Management: AI helps in managing chronic conditions by providing personalized treatment plans that consider an individual's unique health profile.

- Example: For diabetes management, AI systems can recommend personalized diet and exercise plans based on continuous glucose monitoring data.

2. Drug Development and Repurposing:

   o Drug Discovery: AI accelerates the drug discovery process by predicting which compounds are likely to be effective for specific genetic profiles.

      - Example: AI models can analyze the interaction between drugs and genetic variations to identify potential new treatments for rare diseases.

   o Drug Repurposing: AI identifies existing drugs that can be repurposed to treat conditions based on similarities in genetic and molecular profiles.

      - Example: AI has been used to find new uses for existing medications in treating COVID-19 by analyzing their effects on viral proteins.

3. Real-Time Monitoring and Intervention:

   o Remote Patient Monitoring: AI analyzes data from wearable devices and home monitoring systems to provide real-time health insights and alerts.

      - Example: AI can detect early signs of complications in patients with chronic diseases, prompting timely medical intervention.

   o Personal Health Assistants: AI-powered apps provide personalized health advice and reminders based on individual health data and preferences.

      - Example: Virtual health assistants use AI to offer medication reminders and lifestyle tips tailored to a user's health status and goals.

Benefits of AI in Personalized Medicine

1. Enhanced Treatment Efficacy:

   o Precision: Personalized treatments are more likely to be effective as they are tailored to the specific genetic and molecular characteristics of the patient.

   o Reduced Side Effects: By selecting the most appropriate treatments, AI minimizes the risk of adverse reactions and side effects.

2. Improved Patient Outcomes:

   o Early Detection: AI enables the early identification of diseases, allowing for interventions that can prevent or mitigate severe outcomes.

   o Optimized Management: Continuous monitoring and personalized recommendations help in effectively managing chronic conditions and improving quality of life.

3. Cost Efficiency:

   o Reduced Trial and Error: Personalized medicine reduces the need for trial-and-error approaches in treatment selection, saving time and resources.

   o Preventive Care: Early detection and intervention can prevent the progression of diseases, reducing long-term healthcare costs.

4. Empowered Patients:

   o Personalized Insights: Patients receive tailored health insights and recommendations, increasing their engagement and adherence to treatment plans.

   o Proactive Health Management: AI empowers patients to take a proactive role in managing their health through continuous monitoring and personalized advice.

Challenges and Considerations

1. Data Privacy and Security:

   o Protecting Sensitive Information: Ensuring the confidentiality and security of genetic and health data is paramount.

   o Regulatory Compliance: Adhering to healthcare regulations such as HIPAA to protect patient privacy.

2. Ethical and Bias Concerns:

   o Algorithmic Bias: Addressing biases in AI models to ensure equitable and fair treatment for all patients.

   o Ethical Considerations: Ensuring the ethical use of AI in personalized medicine, including informed consent and transparency.

3. Integration and Adoption:

   o Clinical Workflow Integration: Seamlessly integrating AI tools into existing clinical workflows to enhance, rather than disrupt, healthcare delivery.

   o Provider Acceptance: Gaining the trust and acceptance of healthcare providers to adopt AI-driven personalized medicine approaches.

AI in Healthcare: Challenges and Future Directions

The application of Artificial Intelligence (AI) in healthcare holds immense promise for improving patient outcomes, optimizing clinical workflows, and reducing costs. However, the integration of AI technologies also presents several challenges that need to be addressed to fully realize their potential. Understanding these challenges and exploring future directions are crucial for the successful implementation of AI in healthcare.

Challenges of AI in Healthcare

1. Data Privacy and Security:

   - Sensitive Information: Healthcare data is highly sensitive and personal. Ensuring the confidentiality, integrity, and availability of patient data is paramount.

   - Regulatory Compliance: Compliance with data protection regulations such as the Health Insurance Portability and Accountability Act (HIPAA) in the U.S. and the General Data Protection Regulation (GDPR) in Europe is essential.

   - Cybersecurity Threats: AI systems can be vulnerable to cyber-attacks, which can compromise patient data and disrupt healthcare services.

2. Data Quality and Accessibility:

   - Data Heterogeneity: Healthcare data comes from diverse sources and formats, making it challenging to integrate and standardize.

   - Incomplete and Inaccurate Data: Missing, inconsistent, or erroneous data can affect the accuracy and reliability of AI models.

   - Interoperability Issues: Lack of interoperability between different healthcare systems and data silos hampers the seamless exchange of information.

3. Algorithmic Bias and Fairness:

o Bias in Data: AI models trained on biased data can perpetuate and even amplify existing disparities in healthcare.

o Equitable Access: Ensuring that AI benefits all populations, including underrepresented and marginalized groups, is critical to avoid exacerbating health inequities.

o Transparency and Accountability: Ensuring that AI decision-making processes are transparent and accountable is necessary to build trust among healthcare providers and patients.

4. Clinical Integration and Workflow:

o User Acceptance: Healthcare providers may be hesitant to adopt AI tools due to concerns about reliability, usability, and impact on their practice.

o Workflow Disruption: Integrating AI into clinical workflows without causing disruption or increasing the burden on healthcare professionals is challenging.

o Training and Education: Adequate training and education for healthcare professionals on the use and benefits of AI are crucial for successful implementation.

5. Ethical and Legal Considerations:

o Informed Consent: Ensuring that patients are fully informed about the use of AI in their care and obtaining their consent is essential.

o Accountability for AI Decisions: Determining who is responsible for decisions made by AI systems, especially in cases of errors or adverse outcomes, is a complex issue.

o Ethical Use of AI: Ensuring that AI is used ethically, with a focus on patient welfare and social good, is a fundamental challenge.

Future Directions of AI in Healthcare

1. Advanced Data Integration and Interoperability:

- Unified Data Standards: Developing and adopting standardized data formats and protocols to facilitate seamless data exchange across different systems.

- Interoperable Health Information Systems: Creating interoperable systems that allow for the integration and analysis of data from multiple sources, including EHRs, wearable devices, and genomic databases.

2. Enhancing Data Privacy and Security:

- Robust Encryption Techniques: Implementing advanced encryption methods to protect patient data from unauthorized access and breaches.

- Secure AI Models: Developing AI models that are resilient to cyber-attacks and can maintain data privacy while processing sensitive information.

- Regulatory Frameworks: Strengthening regulatory frameworks to ensure the safe and ethical use of AI in healthcare.

3. Addressing Bias and Ensuring Fairness:

- Diverse and Representative Datasets: Ensuring that training datasets are diverse and representative of all population groups to minimize bias.

- Bias Detection and Mitigation: Developing techniques to detect and mitigate bias in AI models, ensuring equitable outcomes for all patients.

- Transparency and Explainability: Creating AI models that are transparent and explainable, allowing healthcare providers and patients to understand and trust AI decisions.

4. Improving Clinical Integration and Adoption:

- User-Friendly Interfaces: Designing AI tools with intuitive, user-friendly interfaces that integrate seamlessly into clinical workflows.

- o Collaborative AI Systems: Developing AI systems that work collaboratively with healthcare providers, enhancing their capabilities rather than replacing them.

- o Continuous Education and Training: Providing ongoing education and training for healthcare professionals to increase their confidence and competence in using AI technologies.

5. Ethical and Legal Frameworks:

- o Ethical Guidelines: Establishing ethical guidelines for the development and use of AI in healthcare, focusing on patient safety, privacy, and welfare.

- o Legal Accountability: Developing legal frameworks that clearly define accountability and liability for AI-driven decisions and outcomes.

- o Patient-Centric AI: Ensuring that AI systems prioritize patient-centric care, respecting patient autonomy and individual rights.

AI in Business and Finance

AI in Business and Finance: Predictive Analytics

Predictive analytics is a powerful application of AI that is transforming business and finance by leveraging data to forecast future trends, behaviors, and events. By utilizing sophisticated algorithms and machine learning techniques, predictive analytics enables organizations to make informed decisions, optimize operations, and gain a competitive edge. Here's an in-depth look at the role and impact of predictive analytics in business and finance.

Key Concepts of Predictive Analytics

1. Data Collection and Integration:

    o Historical Data: Aggregating past data from various sources such as sales records, market trends, financial statements, and customer interactions.

    o Real-Time Data: Incorporating real-time data streams, including social media activity, transaction data, and IoT sensor data, for timely analysis.

2. Machine Learning Algorithms:

    o Regression Analysis: Modeling the relationship between dependent and independent variables to predict future outcomes.

    o Classification Algorithms: Categorizing data into predefined classes to identify patterns and predict categorical outcomes.

    o Time Series Analysis: Analyzing sequential data points to forecast future values and trends over time.

3. Data Preprocessing:

    o Data Cleaning: Removing inaccuracies, inconsistencies, and missing values to ensure data quality.

    o Feature Selection: Identifying and selecting relevant variables that contribute significantly to predictive accuracy.

- o Normalization and Scaling: Transforming data to a common scale to improve algorithm performance.

4. Model Training and Validation:

   - o Training Data: Using a subset of the data to train predictive models and learn patterns.

   - o Validation Data: Evaluating the model's performance on unseen data to ensure generalizability and prevent overfitting.

Applications of Predictive Analytics in Business

1. Customer Relationship Management (CRM):

   - o Customer Segmentation: Identifying distinct customer groups based on purchasing behavior, preferences, and demographics.

   - o Churn Prediction: Predicting which customers are likely to leave and developing strategies to retain them.

   - o Personalized Marketing: Creating targeted marketing campaigns based on individual customer preferences and behavior.

2. Sales and Marketing:

   - o Sales Forecasting: Predicting future sales volumes based on historical data and market trends.

   - o Lead Scoring: Ranking potential customers based on their likelihood to convert into paying customers.

   - o Campaign Effectiveness: Evaluating the impact of marketing campaigns and optimizing them for better ROI.

3. Supply Chain Management:

   - o Demand Forecasting: Predicting product demand to optimize inventory levels and reduce stockouts or overstock situations.

   - o Supplier Performance Analysis: Assessing supplier reliability and performance to make informed procurement decisions.

- o Logistics Optimization: Forecasting shipping times and identifying potential disruptions in the supply chain.

Applications of Predictive Analytics in Finance

1. Risk Management:

   - o Credit Scoring: Predicting the likelihood of a borrower defaulting on a loan based on historical credit data and financial behavior.

   - o Fraud Detection: Identifying fraudulent transactions by analyzing patterns and anomalies in transaction data.

   - o Market Risk Assessment: Evaluating potential market risks and their impact on investment portfolios.

2. Investment Strategies:

   - o Algorithmic Trading: Developing trading algorithms that predict market movements and execute trades automatically based on predefined criteria.

   - o Portfolio Optimization: Using predictive models to balance risk and return, ensuring optimal asset allocation.

   - o Sentiment Analysis: Analyzing social media and news sentiment to predict market reactions and investment opportunities.

3. Financial Planning and Forecasting:

   - o Cash Flow Forecasting: Predicting future cash flows to manage liquidity and financial planning effectively.

   - o Revenue Forecasting: Estimating future revenues based on historical sales data, market conditions, and economic indicators.

   - o Expense Management: Predicting future expenses to optimize budgeting and cost control.

Benefits of Predictive Analytics

1. Improved Decision-Making:

- o Data-Driven Insights: Enabling organizations to make informed decisions based on data analysis and predictive modeling.

- o Proactive Strategies: Allowing businesses to anticipate future trends and take proactive measures to capitalize on opportunities or mitigate risks.

2. Enhanced Efficiency:

- o Operational Optimization: Streamlining business processes and improving operational efficiency through accurate forecasting and resource allocation.

- o Cost Savings: Reducing costs by optimizing inventory levels, minimizing wastage, and preventing fraud.

3. Competitive Advantage:

- o Market Insights: Gaining a deeper understanding of market dynamics and customer behavior, providing a competitive edge.

- o Innovation: Leveraging predictive analytics to identify emerging trends and innovate products or services accordingly.

Challenges and Considerations

1. Data Quality and Management:

- o Data Accuracy: Ensuring the accuracy and completeness of data used for predictive modeling is crucial.

- o Data Integration: Integrating data from multiple sources and systems can be challenging and requires robust data management practices.

2. Model Complexity and Interpretability:

- o Complex Algorithms: Some predictive models, especially those using deep learning, can be complex and difficult to interpret.

- o Explainability: Ensuring that predictive models are transparent and their predictions can be explained to stakeholders is important for trust and adoption.

3. Ethical and Legal Considerations:

- o Bias and Fairness: Addressing potential biases in predictive models to ensure fair and equitable outcomes.

- o Privacy Concerns: Ensuring compliance with data privacy regulations and protecting sensitive customer information.

Future Directions of Predictive Analytics

1. Advancements in AI and Machine Learning:

- o Improved Algorithms: Developing more sophisticated and accurate predictive algorithms to enhance forecasting capabilities.

- o Automated Machine Learning (AutoML): Leveraging AutoML to automate the process of model selection, training, and tuning, making predictive analytics more accessible.

2. Integration with Big Data Technologies:

- o Scalable Solutions: Utilizing big data technologies to handle large volumes of data and perform real-time predictive analytics.

- o Cloud Computing: Leveraging cloud-based platforms to provide scalable, flexible, and cost-effective predictive analytics solutions.

3. Interdisciplinary Approaches:

- o Combining Disciplines: Integrating insights from various disciplines, including economics, psychology, and behavioral science, to enhance predictive models.

- o Collaborative Ecosystems: Fostering collaboration between data scientists, domain experts, and business leaders to create holistic and effective predictive solutions.

AI in Business and Finance: Customer Service Automation

AI-driven customer service automation is revolutionizing the way businesses interact with their customers. By employing advanced technologies such as chatbots, virtual assistants, and machine learning algorithms, organizations can provide efficient, personalized, and scalable customer support. This transformation not only enhances customer satisfaction but also optimizes operational efficiency.

Key Components of AI in Customer Service Automation

1. Chatbots:

   - Rule-Based Chatbots: Operate on predefined scripts and rules to handle common customer queries.

     - Example: Answering frequently asked questions about store hours, return policies, and product details.

   - AI-Powered Chatbots: Utilize natural language processing (NLP) and machine learning to understand and respond to more complex queries.

     - Example: Assisting customers with troubleshooting issues, booking appointments, and providing personalized recommendations.

2. Virtual Assistants:

   - Voice Assistants: Respond to voice commands and provide hands-free customer support.

     - Example: Amazon's Alexa, Google Assistant, and Apple's Siri can help customers check account balances, pay bills, and retrieve information.

   - Text-Based Assistants: Interact with customers through messaging platforms, offering real-time support.

- Example: Virtual assistants embedded in banking apps that help customers with transactions and financial advice.

3. Machine Learning Algorithms:

   o Sentiment Analysis: Analyzes customer interactions to gauge sentiment and adjust responses accordingly.

     - Example: Identifying customer frustration and escalating the issue to a human agent for resolution.

   o Recommendation Systems: Suggests products, services, or solutions based on customer preferences and behaviors.

     - Example: Personalized product recommendations on e-commerce platforms based on past purchases and browsing history.

4. Automated Email Responses:

   o Template-Based Responses: Automatically generates responses for common queries using predefined templates.

     - Example: Sending confirmation emails for orders, bookings, and service requests.

   o AI-Enhanced Email Handling: Analyzes the content of emails to provide relevant responses and route more complex inquiries to human agents.

     - Example: Using NLP to understand the context of customer emails and provide accurate, context-specific replies.

Benefits of AI in Customer Service Automation

1. Enhanced Customer Experience:

   o 24/7 Availability: AI-powered customer service solutions provide round-the-clock support, ensuring that customers can get assistance anytime.

- Quick Response Times: Automated systems can handle multiple inquiries simultaneously, significantly reducing wait times.

- Personalization: AI algorithms analyze customer data to provide personalized responses and recommendations, enhancing the customer experience.

2. Operational Efficiency:

- Cost Reduction: Automating routine tasks reduces the need for extensive human resources, leading to significant cost savings.

- Scalability: AI systems can easily scale to handle increased customer service demands without additional staffing.

- Consistent Service Quality: AI ensures consistent service quality by providing standardized responses to common queries.

3. Data-Driven Insights:

- Customer Behavior Analysis: AI tools analyze customer interactions to identify trends, preferences, and pain points.

- Performance Monitoring: Track and measure the performance of customer service operations, enabling continuous improvement.

- Predictive Insights: AI can predict customer needs and behaviors, allowing businesses to proactively address issues and offer solutions.

Challenges of AI in Customer Service Automation

1. Complex Query Handling:

- Limitations of AI: While AI is proficient at handling simple and repetitive tasks, it may struggle with complex and nuanced customer inquiries.

- Seamless Handoff: Ensuring a smooth transition from AI to human agents when complex issues arise is critical to maintaining customer satisfaction.

2. Data Privacy and Security:

   - ○ Sensitive Information: Handling and storing customer data securely to comply with data protection regulations.

   - ○ Trust Issues: Ensuring that customers trust AI systems with their personal information and interactions.

3. Maintaining a Human Touch:

   - ○ Personal Connection: Balancing automation with the need for human interaction to maintain a personal connection with customers.

   - ○ Customer Preferences: Some customers may prefer human interaction, and businesses need to provide options to accommodate these preferences.

4. Implementation and Maintenance:

   - ○ Integration with Existing Systems: Seamlessly integrating AI tools with existing customer service platforms and workflows.

   - ○ Continuous Improvement: Regularly updating and refining AI systems to keep up with evolving customer needs and technological advancements.

Future Directions of AI in Customer Service Automation

1. Advanced Natural Language Processing:

   - ○ Improved Understanding: Enhancing NLP capabilities to better understand and respond to complex customer queries.

   - ○ Multilingual Support: Expanding language support to cater to a global customer base.

2. Proactive Customer Support:

   - ○ Predictive Analytics: Using predictive analytics to anticipate customer needs and provide proactive support.

- o Automated Follow-Ups: Implementing systems that automatically follow up with customers after interactions to ensure satisfaction.

3. Integration with Other Technologies:

   - o IoT Integration: Leveraging data from IoT devices to provide contextual and timely customer support.

   - o Augmented Reality (AR): Using AR to provide interactive and immersive customer support experiences.

4. Enhanced Personalization:

   - o Behavioral Insights: Using AI to gain deeper insights into customer behavior and preferences for highly personalized interactions.

   - o Dynamic Customer Profiles: Creating dynamic and evolving customer profiles that update in real-time based on interactions and behaviors.

5. Ethical AI Development:

   - o Bias Mitigation: Developing AI systems that are fair and unbiased in their interactions with customers.

   - o Transparency: Ensuring transparency in AI decision-making processes to build trust with customers.

AI in Business and Finance: Fraud Detection

Fraud detection is a critical application of AI in the business and finance sectors. With the increasing complexity and volume of transactions, traditional methods of detecting fraud are becoming less effective. AI and machine learning offer sophisticated solutions that can analyze vast amounts of data in real-time, identify patterns, and detect anomalies that may indicate fraudulent activities. This approach enhances the accuracy and efficiency of fraud detection, ultimately protecting businesses and consumers from financial losses.

Key Components of AI in Fraud Detection

1. Data Collection and Integration:

   o Transaction Data: Collecting data from various financial transactions, including credit card payments, online purchases, and wire transfers.

   o Behavioral Data: Monitoring user behavior, such as login times, transaction patterns, and device usage.

   o External Data: Integrating data from external sources like blacklists, known fraud databases, and social media.

2. Machine Learning Algorithms:

   o Supervised Learning: Training models on labeled datasets where instances of fraud and non-fraud are clearly marked.

      ▪ Examples: Logistic regression, decision trees, and support vector machines.

   o Unsupervised Learning: Identifying patterns and anomalies in unlabeled data without prior knowledge of fraud instances.

      ▪ Examples: Clustering algorithms like K-means and hierarchical clustering, and anomaly detection techniques.

   o Semi-Supervised Learning: Combining both labeled and unlabeled data to improve detection accuracy.

3. Real-Time Analytics:

   o Streaming Data Analysis: Continuously analyzing transaction data in real-time to detect and respond to fraudulent activities as they occur.

   o Automated Alerts: Triggering automated alerts and actions, such as blocking transactions or flagging accounts, when suspicious activities are detected.

Benefits of AI in Fraud Detection

1. Enhanced Accuracy:

   o Pattern Recognition: AI algorithms can identify complex patterns and correlations that are often missed by traditional rule-based systems.

   o Reduced False Positives: Machine learning models can minimize false positives by more accurately distinguishing between legitimate and fraudulent activities.

2. Efficiency and Scalability:

   o Processing Speed: AI systems can process and analyze large volumes of data much faster than human analysts.

   o Scalability: AI solutions can scale easily to handle increasing transaction volumes without significant additional costs.

3. Adaptive Learning:

   o Continuous Improvement: Machine learning models can continuously learn and adapt to new fraud patterns as they emerge.

   o Dynamic Updates: AI systems can be updated in real-time to incorporate new data and improve detection capabilities.

4. Cost Savings:

- o Resource Optimization: Automating fraud detection reduces the need for extensive manual review processes, saving time and resources.

- o Loss Prevention: Early detection of fraud can prevent significant financial losses and protect the organization's reputation.

Challenges of AI in Fraud Detection

1. Data Quality and Availability:

   - o Incomplete Data: Ensuring that all relevant data is collected and integrated for comprehensive analysis.

   - o Data Privacy: Balancing the need for data access with privacy concerns and regulatory compliance.

2. Algorithm Bias:

   - o Bias in Training Data: Ensuring that training data is representative and free from biases that could lead to unfair treatment of certain customer groups.

   - o Fairness and Ethics: Developing algorithms that are fair and ethical in their detection and decision-making processes.

3. Complex Fraud Tactics:

   - o Evolving Fraud Techniques: Staying ahead of increasingly sophisticated and evolving fraud tactics.

   - o Adaptability: Ensuring that AI systems can quickly adapt to new fraud schemes and tactics.

4. False Positives and Negatives:

   - o Balancing Accuracy: Striking the right balance between false positives (legitimate transactions flagged as fraud) and false negatives (fraudulent transactions not detected).

   - o Customer Experience: Minimizing disruptions to legitimate customer activities while ensuring robust fraud protection.

Future Directions of AI in Fraud Detection

1. Advanced Machine Learning Techniques:

   o Deep Learning: Utilizing deep learning models to analyze complex data structures and improve detection accuracy.

   o Hybrid Models: Combining multiple machine learning approaches to enhance overall performance and robustness.

2. Behavioral Biometrics:

   o User Behavior Analysis: Analyzing unique user behaviors, such as typing patterns and mouse movements, to detect anomalies.

   o Continuous Authentication: Implementing continuous authentication mechanisms that monitor user behavior throughout the session.

3. Explainable AI (XAI):

   o Transparency: Developing AI models that provide clear explanations for their decisions to build trust and ensure regulatory compliance.

   o Interpretability: Ensuring that fraud detection systems are interpretable by human analysts for effective validation and action.

4. Integration with Blockchain:

   o Immutable Records: Leveraging blockchain technology to create immutable and transparent transaction records, making it harder for fraudsters to alter or falsify data.

   o Smart Contracts: Using smart contracts to automate and enforce fraud prevention measures in real-time.

Part V: Ethical, Legal, and Social Implications

Ethical Considerations in AI: Bias and Fairness

As artificial intelligence (AI) becomes increasingly integrated into various aspects of society, addressing ethical considerations, particularly those related to bias and fairness, is paramount. AI systems are powerful tools that can make decisions affecting many aspects of human life, from hiring practices to loan approvals and criminal justice. Ensuring that these systems operate fairly and without bias is crucial for maintaining trust and promoting equity.

Understanding Bias in AI

1. Definition of Bias:

    o Algorithmic Bias: Occurs when an AI system produces systematically prejudiced results due to erroneous assumptions in the machine learning process.

    o Data Bias: Arises when the data used to train AI models is not representative of the target population or contains inherent prejudices.

2. Sources of Bias:

    o Historical Bias: Reflects and perpetuates past inequalities present in historical data.

    o Selection Bias: Results from non-representative training data, leading to skewed outcomes.

    o Measurement Bias: Occurs when the data collection process inaccurately measures the attributes of interest.

    o Algorithmic Bias: Introduced through the design and implementation of the AI algorithms, often unintentionally.

Fairness in AI

1. Definition of Fairness:

    o Equitable Treatment: Ensuring that AI systems treat all individuals and groups fairly, without discrimination.

- o Equal Opportunity: Guaranteeing that all individuals have equal chances for favorable outcomes, irrespective of their demographic attributes.

2. Approaches to Fairness:

- o Group Fairness: Ensuring that different demographic groups are treated similarly.

  - Example: Ensuring that loan approval rates are consistent across different racial groups.

- o Individual Fairness: Treating similar individuals similarly.

  - Example: Ensuring that two individuals with similar credit histories receive similar loan offers.

- o Subgroup Fairness: Addressing fairness within subgroups of the population to prevent more nuanced forms of bias.

  - Example: Ensuring fairness among different age groups within a specific racial demographic.

Challenges in Addressing Bias and Fairness

1. Complexity of Fairness:

   o Multifaceted Nature: Fairness is a multifaceted concept with no one-size-fits-all solution, making it challenging to define and measure.

   o Trade-offs: Balancing fairness across multiple dimensions often involves trade-offs, as improving fairness for one group may inadvertently affect another.

2. Data Limitations:

   o Data Quality: High-quality, representative data is essential for training fair AI systems, but such data is often scarce or difficult to obtain.

   o Historical Prejudices: Historical data may contain embedded biases that perpetuate inequalities in AI models.

3. Algorithm Design:

   o Complex Models: Ensuring fairness in complex machine learning models, such as deep neural networks, is technically challenging.

   o Transparency and Interpretability: Many AI models are "black boxes" that lack transparency, making it difficult to identify and mitigate biases.

Strategies for Mitigating Bias and Ensuring Fairness

1. Data Strategies:

   o Diverse Data Collection: Ensuring that training data is diverse and representative of all demographic groups.

   o Bias Detection and Correction: Implementing techniques to detect and correct biases in data before model training.

2. Algorithmic Approaches:

- o Fairness Constraints: Incorporating fairness constraints and objectives into the machine learning algorithms during the training process.

- o Bias Mitigation Techniques: Applying techniques such as re-weighting, re-sampling, and adversarial debiasing to reduce biases in AI models.

3. Evaluation and Monitoring:

- o Regular Audits: Conducting regular audits and evaluations of AI systems to identify and address biases.

- o Performance Metrics: Developing and using fairness-aware performance metrics to evaluate AI models.

4. Transparency and Accountability:

- o Explainable AI: Designing AI systems that are transparent and interpretable, allowing stakeholders to understand decision-making processes.

- o Accountability Frameworks: Establishing frameworks to hold AI developers and organizations accountable for the fairness of their systems.

5. Regulatory and Ethical Guidelines:

- o Adherence to Standards: Following ethical guidelines and regulatory standards for AI development and deployment.

- o Ethical AI Principles: Embedding ethical principles, such as fairness, accountability, and transparency, into the AI development lifecycle.

Future Directions

1. Advanced Fairness Techniques:

- o Context-Aware Fairness: Developing context-aware fairness techniques that consider the specific application and its societal impact.

- ○ Dynamic Fairness: Creating AI systems that can dynamically adjust to changing fairness requirements over time.

2. Collaborative Efforts:

   - ○ Interdisciplinary Research: Promoting interdisciplinary research to address bias and fairness from multiple perspectives, including ethics, law, and social sciences.

   - ○ Stakeholder Involvement: Engaging diverse stakeholders, including marginalized communities, in the AI development process to ensure inclusive and fair outcomes.

3. Regulatory Evolution:

   - ○ Evolving Regulations: Developing and updating regulatory frameworks to keep pace with advancements in AI and address emerging fairness issues.

   - ○ Global Standards: Establishing global standards for fairness in AI to ensure consistency and protect against biased outcomes across different regions.

The Social Impact of AI

The Social Impact of AI on Employment and the Future of Work

Artificial intelligence (AI) is reshaping the landscape of work, with profound implications for employment patterns, job roles, and the overall economy. While AI promises increased efficiency, productivity, and innovation, its adoption also raises concerns about job displacement, skills mismatches, and socioeconomic inequalities. Understanding the social impact of AI on employment is crucial for navigating this transformative era and ensuring that the benefits of AI are equitably distributed across society.

Employment Trends in the Age of AI

1. Automation of Routine Tasks:

    o AI technologies, such as machine learning and robotics, are increasingly capable of automating routine, repetitive tasks across various industries, from manufacturing and transportation to customer service and administration.

    o Jobs most susceptible to automation include those involving predictable physical activities, data processing, and simple decision-making.

2. Creation of New Jobs:

    o While AI may displace certain job roles, it also creates new opportunities for employment in areas such as AI development, data science, cybersecurity, and human-AI collaboration.

    o New job roles often require higher levels of technical skills, digital literacy, and problem-solving abilities, leading to shifts in workforce composition and skill requirements.

3. Transformation of Existing Roles:

- o AI augments human capabilities and transforms job roles by automating routine tasks, enabling workers to focus on higher-value activities that require creativity, critical thinking, and emotional intelligence.

- o Jobs that involve complex cognitive tasks, interpersonal interactions, and adaptability are less likely to be fully automated and may experience changes in job tasks and skill requirements.

Socioeconomic Impacts of AI on Employment

1. Job Displacement and Reskilling Challenges:

   - o Displaced workers may face challenges in transitioning to new roles due to skills mismatches, geographic constraints, and structural barriers.

   - o Effective reskilling and upskilling initiatives are essential to equip workers with the skills needed to thrive in the AI-driven economy and mitigate the risk of unemployment and income inequality.

2. Labor Market Polarization:

   - o The adoption of AI technologies contributes to labor market polarization, with job growth concentrated in high-skilled, high-paying occupations and low-skilled, low-paying jobs, while middle-skilled jobs experience decline.

   - o This polarization exacerbates income inequality and socioeconomic disparities, widening the gap between those with advanced skills and those without.

3. Impacts on Workforce Diversity and Inclusion:

   - o AI systems may inherit biases from historical data and exacerbate existing disparities in hiring, promotion, and performance evaluation processes.

- Addressing biases in AI algorithms and promoting diversity and inclusion in AI development and deployment is critical for building fair and equitable workplaces.

Policy and Societal Responses to AI Employment Challenges

1. Education and Lifelong Learning:

    - Investing in education and lifelong learning programs to equip individuals with the skills needed to adapt to technological change and pursue opportunities in emerging industries.

    - Promoting interdisciplinary education that combines technical skills with critical thinking, creativity, and social intelligence.

2. Labor Market Policies and Social Safety Nets:

    - Implementing labor market policies, such as job training programs, unemployment benefits, and income support schemes, to support workers affected by job displacement and economic restructuring.

    - Establishing portable benefits and social safety nets that provide financial security and stability in the gig economy and non-traditional work arrangements.

3. Ethical AI Development and Regulation:

    - Promoting responsible AI development practices that prioritize ethical considerations, transparency, and accountability.

    - Enacting regulations and standards to address the ethical, legal, and social implications of AI on employment, privacy, and human rights.

4. Public-Private Collaboration:

    - Fostering collaboration between governments, businesses, academia, and civil society to develop inclusive policies and initiatives that promote economic resilience, social mobility, and workforce diversity.

- o Encouraging industry-led initiatives to invest in workforce development, apprenticeship programs, and AI literacy campaigns.

The Future of Work in the AI Era

1. Hybrid Workforce Models:

   - o The future of work is likely to involve hybrid workforce models that combine human and AI capabilities, enabling seamless collaboration and task allocation between humans and machines.

   - o Human-AI collaboration platforms and augmented intelligence tools will empower workers to leverage AI technologies to augment their skills and decision-making abilities.

2. Skills-Driven Economy:

   - o The shift towards a skills-driven economy will require continuous learning and adaptability, with an emphasis on digital literacy, data fluency, problem-solving, and interpersonal skills.

   - o Lifelong learning platforms, micro-credentialing systems, and alternative education models will play a vital role in enabling individuals to acquire and update their skills throughout their careers.

3. Redefining Work and Value:

   - o The increasing automation of routine tasks will necessitate a redefinition of work and value, with a greater emphasis on creativity, innovation, human connection, and societal impact.

   - o Jobs that involve empathy, emotional intelligence, caregiving, and social interaction will become increasingly valuable in the AI-driven economy.

The Social Impact of AI in Education

Artificial intelligence (AI) is revolutionizing the field of education, offering transformative opportunities to enhance teaching and learning experiences, personalize education pathways, and address challenges in access and equity. As AI technologies continue to evolve, they have the potential to reshape educational practices, improve student outcomes, and empower educators to meet the diverse needs of learners in the 21st century.

Advancements in AI Education Technologies

1. Personalized Learning:

   o AI-powered adaptive learning platforms analyze students' learning patterns, preferences, and performance data to deliver personalized learning experiences tailored to individual needs and pace.

   o Personalized learning algorithms adjust content, pacing, and instructional strategies in real-time, allowing students to learn at their own pace and mastery level.

2. Intelligent Tutoring Systems:

   o AI-driven tutoring systems provide immediate feedback, guidance, and scaffolding to students as they engage with learning materials, helping them overcome challenges and master concepts more effectively.

   o These systems can diagnose students' misconceptions, adapt instructional strategies, and provide targeted interventions to support personalized learning pathways.

3. Enhanced Teaching and Learning Resources:

- AI technologies enable the creation of interactive and immersive educational resources, such as virtual reality simulations, augmented reality experiences, and intelligent educational games, to engage students and enhance learning outcomes.

- AI-powered content recommendation systems suggest relevant learning materials, videos, and resources based on students' interests, learning styles, and proficiency levels.

Addressing Educational Inequities

1. Access to Quality Education:

   - AI-enabled remote learning platforms and digital educational resources provide access to high-quality education for students in underserved and remote communities, bridging geographical and socioeconomic barriers to learning.

   - AI-driven language translation tools support multilingual learners and learners with disabilities, ensuring inclusivity and accessibility in educational settings.

2. Closing the Achievement Gap:

   - AI-powered adaptive learning technologies can help address disparities in academic achievement by providing targeted interventions and personalized support to students at risk of falling behind.

   - Intelligent tutoring systems offer differentiated instruction and scaffolding to meet the diverse needs of learners, including those with learning disabilities or special educational needs.

Challenges and Considerations

1. Data Privacy and Security:

   - Collecting and analyzing sensitive student data raises concerns about data privacy, security, and ethical use of AI technologies in educational settings.

- o Safeguarding student privacy and ensuring compliance with data protection regulations are paramount considerations for educators, policymakers, and technology developers.

2. Algorithmic Bias and Fairness:

- o AI algorithms may inherit biases from training data, leading to unintended consequences, inequitable outcomes, and perpetuation of stereotypes in educational decision-making.

- o Addressing algorithmic bias requires careful scrutiny of data sources, transparency in algorithm design, and ongoing monitoring and evaluation of AI systems for fairness and equity.

Future Directions and Opportunities

1. Augmented Intelligence in Education:

- o The future of AI in education lies in augmenting human intelligence and expertise rather than replacing human teachers.

- o Collaborative AI technologies empower educators with data-driven insights, instructional recommendations, and personalized support to optimize teaching practices and student learning experiences.

2. Lifelong Learning and Skills Development:

- o AI-driven adaptive learning platforms and lifelong learning ecosystems support continuous skill development, professional growth, and career advancement for learners of all ages.

- o AI technologies can help individuals acquire in-demand skills, adapt to changing job market demands, and navigate lifelong learning pathways in the digital age.

3. Global Collaboration and Knowledge Sharing:

- o Collaborative AI initiatives and international partnerships facilitate knowledge sharing, best practices exchange, and capacity building in AI education research, policy development, and implementation.

- Open educational resources, AI-enabled learning platforms, and online communities of practice foster collaboration and innovation in education on a global scale.

The Social Impact of AI on Societal Change

Artificial Intelligence (AI) is driving profound societal changes across various domains, including healthcare, transportation, finance, governance, and communication. As AI technologies continue to evolve, they are reshaping the ways we work, interact, and live, with far-reaching implications for individuals, communities, and societies at large. Understanding the social impact of AI is crucial for navigating this transformative era and harnessing the potential benefits while addressing emerging challenges and ethical considerations.

Transformative Impacts of AI on Society

1. Automation and Job Displacement:

    - AI-driven automation is transforming industries and job roles, leading to shifts in employment patterns, skill requirements, and workforce dynamics.

    - While AI may create new job opportunities in emerging sectors, it also poses risks of job displacement for workers in routine and repetitive tasks, leading to concerns about unemployment and income inequality.

2. Enhanced Productivity and Efficiency:

    - AI technologies improve productivity, streamline business processes, and optimize resource allocation through data-driven insights, predictive analytics, and automation.

    - Organizations leverage AI-powered tools and systems to enhance decision-making, accelerate innovation, and deliver higher quality products and services to consumers.

3. Personalization and Customization:

- AI enables personalized experiences and tailored recommendations in various domains, including e-commerce, entertainment, education, and healthcare.

- Personalization algorithms analyze user preferences, behavior, and historical data to deliver customized content, services, and recommendations that meet individual needs and preferences.

4. Healthcare Advancements:

- AI-driven innovations in healthcare, such as medical imaging, diagnostics, drug discovery, and personalized medicine, improve patient outcomes, disease management, and healthcare delivery.

- AI algorithms assist clinicians in diagnosis, treatment planning, and patient care, enhancing medical decision-making and reducing diagnostic errors.

5. Transportation and Mobility:

- AI technologies, including autonomous vehicles, traffic management systems, and ride-sharing platforms, revolutionize transportation and mobility, offering safer, more efficient, and sustainable mobility solutions.

- Autonomous vehicles reduce accidents, congestion, and carbon emissions while improving access to transportation for individuals with mobility limitations.

6. Ethical and Societal Challenges:

- AI raises ethical concerns related to privacy, security, fairness, bias, accountability, and transparency in decision-making processes.

- Societal issues, such as algorithmic discrimination, job displacement, surveillance, and loss of human agency, require careful consideration and mitigation strategies to ensure responsible AI development and deployment.

Addressing Ethical and Societal Implications

1. Ethical AI Development:

   - Promoting ethical AI principles, such as fairness, transparency, accountability, and privacy, throughout the AI lifecycle.

   - Integrating ethical considerations into AI design, development, deployment, and governance processes to minimize unintended consequences and societal harms.

2. Regulatory Frameworks and Policies:

   - Enacting regulations, standards, and guidelines to govern the responsible use of AI technologies and mitigate potential risks to individuals, communities, and society.

   - Collaborating with policymakers, industry stakeholders, academia, and civil society to develop adaptive regulatory frameworks that balance innovation with societal interests and values.

3. Public Engagement and Awareness:

   - Fostering public dialogue, awareness, and engagement on AI-related issues to promote informed decision-making, ethical practices, and responsible AI adoption.

   - Educating stakeholders, including policymakers, educators, businesses, and the general public, about the societal impacts of AI, ethical considerations, and potential risks and benefits.

4. Equitable Access and Inclusion:

   - Ensuring equitable access to AI technologies, benefits, and opportunities for individuals from diverse socioeconomic backgrounds, geographic regions, and demographic groups.

   - Addressing digital divides, biases, and barriers to access to ensure that AI benefits are distributed equitably and contribute to societal well-being and inclusive growth.

Future Directions and Opportunities

1. Human-Centric AI Solutions:

    o Designing AI systems that prioritize human well-being, autonomy, and dignity, and enhance human capabilities rather than replace human agency.

    o Emphasizing human-centered design principles, user empowerment, and inclusive technology development processes to build AI technologies that serve societal needs and values.

2. Interdisciplinary Collaboration:

    o Encouraging interdisciplinary collaboration between AI researchers, social scientists, ethicists, policymakers, and stakeholders to address complex societal challenges and foster responsible AI innovation.

    o Integrating diverse perspectives, expertise, and methodologies to develop contextually relevant, culturally sensitive, and ethically informed AI solutions.

3. Global Cooperation and Governance:

    o Promoting international cooperation, collaboration, and knowledge sharing on AI governance, standards, and best practices to address global challenges and ensure ethical AI development and deployment.

    o Establishing multilateral forums, partnerships, and mechanisms for dialogue, capacity building, and coordination on AI-related issues, including ethics, regulation, and human rights.

Part VI: The Future of AI

Trends and Innovations

AI Emerging Technologies

Artificial Intelligence (AI) is a rapidly evolving field that continues to push the boundaries of innovation, revolutionizing industries, and transforming society. As AI technologies mature and new breakthroughs emerge, several trends and innovations are shaping the future of AI development and deployment. From advances in machine learning algorithms to the rise of AI-powered applications and interdisciplinary research collaborations, these trends offer exciting opportunities and challenges for the AI ecosystem.

1. Advancements in Deep Learning

    1. Transformer Architectures: Transformer-based models, such as BERT (Bidirectional Encoder Representations from Transformers) and GPT (Generative Pre-trained Transformer), have demonstrated remarkable performance in natural language processing (NLP), text generation, and language understanding tasks.

    2. Attention Mechanisms: Attention mechanisms improve the interpretability and performance of deep learning models by allowing them to focus on relevant parts of input data, enabling more context-aware and precise predictions.

2. Reinforcement Learning and Self-Supervised Learning

    1. Reinforcement Learning (RL): RL algorithms, such as Deep Q-Networks (DQN) and Proximal Policy Optimization (PPO), are advancing autonomous decision-making in complex environments, including robotics, gaming, and control systems.

    2. Self-Supervised Learning: Self-supervised learning approaches, such as contrastive learning and pretext tasks, enable models to learn meaningful representations from unlabeled data, reducing the need for large annotated datasets.

3. Federated Learning and Edge AI

1. Federated Learning: Federated learning enables collaborative model training across distributed devices and data sources while preserving data privacy and security, making it suitable for applications in healthcare, Internet of Things (IoT), and decentralized environments.

2. Edge AI: Edge computing and AI empower devices to perform computation and inference locally, reducing latency, bandwidth requirements, and dependency on cloud infrastructure, enabling real-time, privacy-preserving AI applications at the network edge.

4. Ethical AI and Responsible Innovation

1. Fairness, Accountability, and Transparency (FAT): Ethical AI frameworks and guidelines promote fairness, accountability, transparency, and interpretability in AI development and deployment, addressing biases, discrimination, and societal impacts.

2. Explainable AI (XAI): XAI techniques enable users to understand and interpret AI models' predictions and decision-making processes, fostering trust, transparency, and human-AI collaboration in critical applications, such as healthcare and finance.

5. AI-Driven Healthcare and Biotechnology

1. Medical Imaging and Diagnosis: AI-powered medical imaging and diagnostic systems improve disease detection, prognosis, and treatment planning in areas such as radiology, pathology, and oncology, enhancing patient care and clinical decision-making.

2. Drug Discovery and Genomics: AI accelerates drug discovery, molecule design, and personalized medicine by analyzing large-scale biological data, predicting drug-target interactions, and identifying novel therapeutic candidates for complex diseases.

6. Autonomous Vehicles and Robotics

1. Self-Driving Cars: Autonomous vehicle technologies leverage AI algorithms, sensor fusion, and computer vision to navigate complex

environments, reduce accidents, and enhance transportation efficiency and safety.

2. Robotics and Automation: AI-powered robots and automation systems revolutionize manufacturing, logistics, and service industries by performing repetitive tasks, handling materials, and interacting with humans in collaborative environments.

7. Quantum Computing and AI

1. Quantum Machine Learning: Quantum computing offers unprecedented computational power and parallelism, enabling quantum machine learning algorithms to solve optimization, simulation, and pattern recognition problems with exponential speedup.

2. Hybrid Quantum-Classical Computing: Hybrid quantum-classical computing architectures combine classical AI algorithms with quantum computing techniques to address combinatorial optimization, cryptography, and AI model training challenges.

Quantum Computing and AI

Quantum computing and artificial intelligence (AI) represent two cutting-edge fields of technology that are poised to revolutionize computing, problem-solving, and data analysis. While each field has made significant advancements independently, the convergence of quantum computing and AI holds immense promise for tackling complex computational challenges that are beyond the capabilities of classical computing. Understanding the intersection of quantum computing and AI opens up new avenues for innovation, discovery, and the development of transformative applications across various domains.

Quantum Computing Basics

1. Quantum Bits (Qubits): Quantum computers use qubits, which leverage quantum phenomena such as superposition and entanglement to represent and manipulate information in multiple states simultaneously.

2. Quantum Supremacy: Quantum supremacy refers to the milestone where a quantum computer outperforms classical computers on a specific computational task, demonstrating the potential for exponential speedup and computational advantage.

3. Quantum Gates and Algorithms: Quantum gates and quantum algorithms, such as Grover's algorithm and Shor's algorithm, exploit quantum parallelism and interference to solve certain problems more efficiently than classical algorithms.

Quantum Computing and AI Applications

1. Optimization Problems: Quantum computing accelerates optimization tasks, including portfolio optimization, logistics planning, and supply chain management, by exploring vast solution spaces and finding near-optimal solutions in polynomial time.

2. Machine Learning and Pattern Recognition: Quantum machine learning algorithms leverage quantum computing techniques to enhance data analysis, pattern recognition, and feature extraction tasks, enabling more efficient processing of large-scale datasets.

3. Quantum Neural Networks: Quantum neural networks and quantum-inspired algorithms enhance deep learning models' training efficiency, generalization capabilities, and robustness to noise, offering potential advantages in image recognition, natural language processing, and generative modeling.

Challenges and Opportunities

1. Hardware Limitations: Quantum computing hardware faces challenges such as qubit decoherence, gate errors, and scalability issues, requiring advancements in quantum error correction, fault tolerance, and qubit coherence times.

2. Algorithm Development: Designing quantum algorithms that harness the unique capabilities of quantum computers and outperform classical algorithms on real-world problems remains a significant research challenge, requiring interdisciplinary expertise in quantum physics, computer science, and mathematics.

3. Hybrid Quantum-Classical Systems: Hybrid quantum-classical computing architectures combine classical AI algorithms with quantum computing techniques to address combinatorial optimization, cryptography, and AI model training challenges, enabling practical applications in the near term.

Future Directions and Implications

1. AI Acceleration: Quantum computing accelerates AI model training, inference, and optimization tasks, unlocking new capabilities for solving complex problems in machine learning, robotics, autonomous systems, and natural language understanding.

2. Drug Discovery and Material Science: Quantum computing enables simulation of molecular structures, chemical reactions, and material properties, accelerating drug discovery, materials design, and optimization processes in pharmaceuticals, chemistry, and materials science.

3. Security and Cryptography: Quantum computing poses both opportunities and challenges for cybersecurity and cryptography, with quantum-resistant

encryption protocols and quantum-enhanced security solutions needed to protect sensitive data and communications in a post-quantum computing era.

Future Research Directions in AI

Artificial Intelligence (AI) research is a dynamic and rapidly evolving field, continually pushing the boundaries of innovation and expanding the frontiers of what AI systems can achieve. As AI technologies mature and new challenges emerge, future research directions are essential to address critical issues, drive breakthroughs, and shape the trajectory of AI development. From advancing AI algorithms and architectures to exploring interdisciplinary collaborations and addressing societal implications, future research in AI encompasses a wide range of exciting opportunities and challenges.

1. Advanced AI Algorithms and Architectures

   1. Explainable AI (XAI): Developing interpretable and transparent AI models and algorithms that enable users to understand and trust AI systems' predictions, decisions, and reasoning processes.

   2. Adversarial Robustness: Enhancing the robustness and security of AI systems against adversarial attacks, manipulation, and vulnerabilities through robust optimization, adversarial training, and defense mechanisms.

   3. Neurosymbolic AI: Integrating symbolic reasoning and knowledge representation techniques with deep learning and neural networks to create hybrid AI systems capable of abstract reasoning, logical inference, and symbolic manipulation.

2. Interdisciplinary Research and Collaborations

   1. AI and Healthcare: Advancing AI-driven healthcare technologies, including medical imaging, disease diagnosis, drug discovery, and personalized medicine, through interdisciplinary collaborations between AI researchers, clinicians, biomedical scientists, and healthcare practitioners.

   2. AI and Sustainability: Leveraging AI to address global sustainability challenges, such as climate change, environmental conservation, renewable energy, and resource optimization, by developing AI-driven solutions for monitoring, prediction, and decision-making.

3. AI and Social Sciences: Bridging the gap between AI and social sciences to study the societal impacts of AI technologies, understand human-AI interactions, and address ethical, legal, and policy implications of AI deployment in diverse social contexts.

3. Ethical AI and Responsible Innovation

1. AI Ethics and Governance: Promoting ethical AI principles, responsible innovation, and AI governance frameworks that prioritize fairness, accountability, transparency, and human values in AI development and deployment.

2. Algorithmic Bias and Fairness: Mitigating algorithmic biases, discrimination, and fairness issues in AI systems by designing fair and unbiased algorithms, addressing data biases, and ensuring equitable representation and decision-making.

3. AI Regulation and Policy: Developing regulatory frameworks, standards, and guidelines for AI governance, data privacy, cybersecurity, and accountability to address emerging risks and societal concerns associated with AI technologies.

4. AI for Social Good and Global Challenges

1. AI for Education: Harnessing AI to improve access to quality education, personalize learning experiences, and address educational inequities by developing AI-driven educational tools, adaptive learning platforms, and intelligent tutoring systems.

2. AI for Humanitarian Aid: Deploying AI technologies for humanitarian purposes, disaster response, and crisis management to support relief efforts, coordinate resources, and assist vulnerable populations in emergencies and humanitarian crises.

3. AI for Sustainable Development: Using AI to achieve the United Nations Sustainable Development Goals (SDGs) by leveraging AI-driven solutions for poverty alleviation, healthcare access, food security, environmental conservation, and inclusive economic growth.

5. Future AI Applications and Paradigms

1. AI-Powered Creativity: Exploring the intersection of AI and creativity to develop AI-driven tools and systems for artistic expression, music composition, storytelling, design innovation, and creative problem-solving.

2. AI-Augmented Human Intelligence: Enhancing human intelligence and cognition through AI-augmented interfaces, cognitive prosthetics, and brain-computer interfaces that enable symbiotic collaboration between humans and AI systems.

3. AI and Quantum Computing: Investigating the synergies between AI and quantum computing to develop quantum-inspired algorithms, quantum machine learning models, and quantum AI applications that harness the computational power of quantum computers.

AI and Human Collaboration

Enhancing human capabilities with AI

1. Augmented Intelligence

    1. Data Processing and Analysis: AI algorithms excel at processing and analyzing large volumes of data, extracting insights, and identifying patterns that may be difficult for humans to discern. By automating data-intensive tasks, AI frees up human cognitive resources for higher-level reasoning and decision-making.

    2. Decision Support Systems: AI-powered decision support systems provide real-time recommendations, predictions, and insights to assist humans in complex decision-making processes. These systems leverage machine learning models, optimization algorithms, and predictive analytics to augment human judgment and improve decision outcomes.

2. Cognitive Enhancement

    1. Memory Augmentation: AI technologies, such as natural language processing (NLP) and machine learning, enable individuals to access and retrieve information from vast knowledge bases, digital archives, and online repositories, enhancing memory recall and information retrieval capabilities.

    2. Problem-Solving Assistance: AI algorithms can assist humans in solving complex problems by generating hypotheses, exploring solution spaces, and evaluating alternatives. From medical diagnosis to scientific research, AI-powered problem-solving tools accelerate innovation and discovery.

3. Skill Development and Training

    1. Personalized Learning: AI-driven adaptive learning platforms tailor educational content, exercises, and assessments to individual learning styles, preferences, and proficiency levels. By providing personalized feedback and adaptive instruction, AI enhances learning outcomes and facilitates skill acquisition.

    2. Simulated Training Environments: AI-powered simulations and virtual reality (VR) environments provide immersive training experiences for skill

development, professional training, and experiential learning. These environments enable individuals to practice and refine their skills in realistic scenarios without real-world consequences.

4. Creativity and Innovation

   1. Creative Assistance: AI tools, such as generative adversarial networks (GANs) and natural language generation (NLG) models, support creative endeavors by generating artistic content, music compositions, and literary works. These tools inspire human creativity and facilitate ideation and brainstorming processes.

   2. Idea Generation and Optimization: AI algorithms assist in idea generation, optimization, and innovation by exploring design spaces, identifying novel concepts, and optimizing parameters. From product design to engineering optimization, AI-driven creativity tools enhance innovation processes.

5. Collaborative Intelligence

   1. Human-AI Collaboration: Collaborative AI systems enable seamless interaction and collaboration between humans and AI agents, leveraging the complementary strengths of both parties. By combining human intuition, creativity, and contextual understanding with AI's analytical capabilities, collaborative intelligence enhances problem-solving and decision-making processes.

   2. Crowdsourcing and Collective Intelligence: AI platforms facilitate crowdsourcing and collective intelligence by aggregating input from diverse individuals, experts, and stakeholders. By harnessing collective wisdom and expertise, AI enhances problem-solving, idea generation, and decision-making at scale.

Collaborative intelligence

1. Personalized Learning Environments

    1. Adaptive Learning Systems: AI-powered adaptive learning platforms analyze learners' performance data, preferences, and progress to deliver personalized learning pathways, recommendations, and feedback. By adapting content, pacing, and instructional strategies to individual needs, AI enhances learning effectiveness and engagement.

    2. Intelligent Tutoring Systems: AI-driven tutoring systems provide individualized support, guidance, and scaffolding to learners as they navigate learning materials and activities. These systems offer real-time feedback, hints, and explanations to help learners overcome challenges, master concepts, and achieve learning objectives.

2. Augmented Content and Resources

    1. AI-Generated Content: AI technologies generate educational content, exercises, and assessments tailored to learners' proficiency levels, interests, and learning objectives. From interactive tutorials to customized quizzes, AI-generated content enhances engagement and facilitates self-paced learning.

    2. Content Recommendation Systems: AI-powered recommendation systems suggest relevant learning materials, resources, and educational opportunities based on learners' preferences, behavior, and learning history. By curating personalized learning playlists and pathways, AI enhances discoverability and accessibility of educational content.

3. Collaborative Problem-Solving

    1. AI-Assisted Collaboration: AI technologies facilitate collaborative problem-solving and teamwork by providing real-time communication, coordination, and task management tools. These tools enable learners to collaborate on projects, share ideas, and co-create solutions across geographic locations and time zones.

2. AI-Powered Feedback and Assessment: AI algorithms analyze collaborative learning interactions, contributions, and outcomes to provide feedback, evaluation, and performance assessment. By assessing individual and group contributions, AI promotes accountability, reflection, and continuous improvement in collaborative learning settings.

4. Lifelong Learning and Skill Development

   1. Continuous Learning Support: AI-driven lifelong learning platforms support individuals in acquiring new skills, staying updated on emerging trends, and adapting to changing job market demands. These platforms offer personalized learning recommendations, microlearning modules, and skill development pathways tailored to learners' career goals and aspirations.

   2. Skill Assessment and Certification: AI technologies assess learners' skills, competencies, and capabilities through automated skill assessment, competency mapping, and certification programs. By recognizing and validating learners' achievements, AI motivates continuous learning and professional development.

5. Ethical Considerations and Human-Centered Design

   1. Ethical AI Practices: Ethical considerations, such as privacy, transparency, fairness, and bias mitigation, are paramount in AI-enabled collaborative learning environments. Ensuring data privacy, informed consent, and algorithmic fairness is essential to building trust and fostering ethical AI adoption in education.

   2. Human-Centered Design: Human-centered design principles emphasize the importance of designing AI-enabled learning systems that prioritize human needs, values, and experiences. By involving learners in the design process and soliciting feedback iteratively, AI systems can better meet learners' expectations and preferences.

Case studies

1. Healthcare

    1. Medical Imaging Diagnosis: AI algorithms assist radiologists in interpreting medical images, such as X-rays, MRIs, and CT scans, to detect abnormalities, diagnose diseases, and recommend treatment options. Case studies demonstrate how AI improves diagnostic accuracy, reduces interpretation time, and enhances patient outcomes in areas such as cancer detection and cardiovascular imaging.

    2. Drug Discovery and Development: AI-driven drug discovery platforms accelerate the identification and optimization of novel therapeutic compounds, target molecules, and drug candidates. By analyzing molecular structures, biological data, and chemical properties, AI systems expedite the drug discovery process and facilitate precision medicine approaches tailored to individual patient needs.

2. Finance

    1. Fraud Detection and Risk Management: AI-powered fraud detection systems analyze transaction data, patterns, and anomalies to identify fraudulent activities, prevent financial losses, and enhance security in banking and financial institutions. Case studies demonstrate how AI reduces false positives, improves detection accuracy, and mitigates financial risks in areas such as credit card fraud and anti-money laundering compliance.

    2. Algorithmic Trading and Portfolio Management: AI algorithms optimize investment strategies, asset allocation, and trading decisions based on market trends, sentiment analysis, and

predictive analytics. Case studies showcase how AI-driven trading algorithms enhance portfolio performance, reduce transaction costs, and mitigate investment risks in volatile financial markets.

3. Education

   1. Personalized Learning Platforms: AI-powered educational platforms deliver personalized learning experiences, adaptive instruction, and targeted interventions to students based on their individual learning styles, preferences, and performance data. Case studies demonstrate how AI improves student engagement, academic achievement, and retention rates by tailoring educational content, assessments, and feedback to learners' needs.

   2. Intelligent Tutoring Systems: AI-driven tutoring systems provide real-time assistance, feedback, and guidance to students as they navigate learning materials and complete assignments. Case studies highlight how AI tutors adapt instructional strategies, provide scaffolding, and assess learning progress to support students in mastering challenging concepts and acquiring new skills.

4. Sustainability

   1. Energy Efficiency and Resource Optimization: AI technologies optimize energy consumption, resource allocation, and operational efficiency in industries, buildings, and transportation systems. Case studies illustrate how AI-driven solutions, such as smart grids, predictive maintenance, and demand forecasting, reduce energy costs, minimize environmental impact, and enhance sustainability.

   2. Environmental Monitoring and Conservation: AI-powered monitoring systems analyze satellite imagery, sensor data, and

3. environmental indicators to monitor ecosystems, biodiversity, and natural resources. Case studies demonstrate how AI supports environmental conservation efforts, wildlife protection, and climate change mitigation through habitat mapping, species identification, and ecological modeling.

Ethical Considerations and Human-Centered Design

1. Ethical AI Practices: AI and human case studies raise ethical considerations related to privacy, fairness, transparency, and accountability in AI deployment. Ensuring ethical AI practices, data privacy protection, and algorithmic transparency is essential to building trust and fostering responsible AI adoption in diverse applications.

2. Human-Centered Design: Human-centered design principles emphasize the importance of designing AI systems that prioritize human needs, values, and experiences. By involving stakeholders in the design process, soliciting feedback iteratively, and addressing user concerns, AI solutions can better meet human expectations and enhance user satisfaction and acceptance.

Speculative Futures: AGI and Beyond

The quest for Artificial General Intelligence (AGI)

"Speculative Futures: AGI and Beyond" is an exploration into the potential advancements, implications, and ethical considerations surrounding Artificial General Intelligence (AGI) and its evolution beyond human-level intelligence. This examination includes technological challenges, societal impacts, ethical frameworks, and governance mechanisms.

1. Artificial General Intelligence (AGI)

Definition: AGI refers to a type of AI that possesses the ability to understand, learn, and apply knowledge across a wide range of tasks and domains, exhibiting cognitive abilities akin to human intelligence. Unlike narrow AI, which specializes in specific tasks, AGI aims to perform any intellectual task that a human can do.

Significance: The development of AGI represents a monumental leap in AI, promising unprecedented advancements in technology and capabilities that could transform various sectors, including healthcare, education, industry, and beyond.

2. Speculative Futures

Concept: Speculative futures involve envisioning potential scenarios and outcomes that could arise from the development and implementation of AGI. This speculative exercise helps stakeholders anticipate the societal, ethical, and existential ramifications of AGI, guiding proactive discussions and preparations.

3. Challenges and Opportunities

Technological Challenges:

- Complexity of Human Cognition: Understanding and replicating the intricate workings of the human brain remains a significant challenge.
- Scalability: Developing scalable algorithms that can handle diverse and complex tasks across different domains.
- Safety and Reliability: Ensuring that AGI systems operate safely and reliably without unintended consequences.

Ethical Considerations:

- Bias and Fairness: Mitigating biases in AGI systems to ensure fair and equitable outcomes.

- Privacy: Protecting personal data and ensuring privacy in AGI applications.

- Control and Autonomy: Maintaining human control over AGI systems and ensuring they act in accordance with human values and intentions.

Economic and Social Impact:

- Job Displacement: Addressing potential job losses due to automation and ensuring a just transition for affected workers.

- Innovation and Productivity: Harnessing AGI to drive innovation, improve productivity, and solve complex global challenges.

- Inequality: Preventing the exacerbation of social and economic inequalities resulting from unequal access to AGI technologies.

4. Beyond Human-Level Intelligence

Technological Singularity:

- Definition: A hypothetical future point where AI surpasses human intelligence, leading to rapid and unpredictable technological growth.

- Implications: The singularity could bring about profound changes, both positive and negative, in society and human existence.

Friendly vs. Unfriendly AGI:

- Friendly AGI: An AGI that aligns with human values, prioritizing human well-being and ethical considerations.

- Unfriendly AGI: An AGI that could act contrary to human interests, potentially posing significant risks to humanity.

Existential Risks:

- Potential Threats: The development of superintelligent AGI could pose existential threats, including the possibility of AGI systems making decisions that endanger human survival.

- Risk Mitigation: Developing robust safety protocols and ethical frameworks to mitigate these risks and ensure AGI benefits humanity.

5. Ethical Frameworks and Governance

Value Alignment: Ensuring AGI systems are designed and programmed to align with human values and ethical principles.

Safety and Control: Implementing safeguards and control mechanisms to prevent unintended consequences and ensure the safe operation of AGI systems.

Transparency and Accountability: Promoting transparency in AGI development and decision-making processes to build public trust and ensure accountability.

International Cooperation: Fostering global collaboration and dialogue to address the challenges and opportunities of AGI development, ensuring that its benefits are widely shared.

6. Research and Collaboration

Interdisciplinary Research: Encouraging collaboration across various fields, including computer science, neuroscience, ethics, and social sciences, to address the multifaceted challenges of AGI development.

Stakeholder Engagement: Engaging diverse stakeholders, including policymakers, industry leaders, academics, and the public, in discussions about the future of AGI and its societal implications.

Risk Mitigation Strategies: Developing strategies to identify and mitigate potential risks associated with AGI, ensuring that its development proceeds in a safe and ethical manner.

Legal and Regulatory Aspects of AI: A Detailed Exploration

As artificial intelligence (AI) continues to evolve and integrate into various aspects of society, its legal and regulatory landscape becomes increasingly important. The legal and regulatory aspects of AI encompass a wide range of issues, including data protection, ethical considerations, accountability, liability, and the creation of new laws and regulations to manage AI's impact. This detailed exploration covers key areas and challenges in the legal and regulatory domain of AI.

1. Data Protection and Privacy

Key Issues:

- Data Collection: AI systems often require large amounts of data to function effectively. This raises concerns about the methods of data collection, consent, and the potential for misuse of personal data.

- Data Security: Ensuring that data used by AI systems is stored and processed securely to prevent unauthorized access and breaches.

- Compliance with Regulations: Adhering to data protection laws such as the General Data Protection Regulation (GDPR) in Europe, which sets stringent requirements for data handling, consent, and individual rights.

Challenges:

- Balancing Innovation and Privacy: Creating regulations that protect privacy without stifling technological innovation.

- Global Standards: Harmonizing data protection standards across different jurisdictions to facilitate international cooperation and data sharing.

2. Ethical Considerations

Key Issues:

- Bias and Fairness: Addressing biases in AI algorithms that can lead to unfair treatment of individuals or groups.

- Transparency and Explainability: Ensuring that AI decision-making processes are transparent and can be understood by humans.

- Ethical AI Development: Promoting the development of AI systems that adhere to ethical principles, such as beneficence, non-maleficence, autonomy, and justice.

Challenges:

- Defining Ethical Standards: Establishing clear and universally accepted ethical standards for AI development and deployment.

- Enforcement: Implementing effective mechanisms to enforce ethical guidelines and standards.

3. Accountability and Liability

Key Issues:

- Responsibility for AI Actions: Determining who is accountable when an AI system causes harm or makes a mistake.

- Legal Personhood: Debating whether AI systems should be granted some form of legal personhood or if accountability should always rest with the developers and operators.

Challenges:

- Complexity of AI Systems: The complexity and opacity of some AI systems make it difficult to assign accountability clearly.

- Dynamic Regulation: Adapting legal frameworks to keep pace with rapid advancements in AI technology.

4. Creation of New Laws and Regulations

Key Issues:

- Regulatory Frameworks: Developing comprehensive regulatory frameworks that address the unique challenges posed by AI.

- International Cooperation: Facilitating international cooperation to create consistent and harmonized regulations that can be applied globally.

Challenges:

- Balancing Regulation and Innovation: Creating laws that protect public interests without hindering technological progress.

- Future-Proofing Regulations: Ensuring that regulations can adapt to future developments in AI technology and applications.

5. Sector-Specific Regulations

Healthcare:

- Medical Devices and AI: Regulating AI systems used in medical devices to ensure they meet safety and efficacy standards.

- Patient Privacy: Protecting patient data and ensuring compliance with health privacy laws.

Finance:

- Algorithmic Trading: Regulating AI systems used in trading to prevent market manipulation and ensure financial stability.

- Fraud Detection: Ensuring that AI systems used for fraud detection comply with privacy and security regulations.

Transportation:

- Autonomous Vehicles: Developing regulations for the safe deployment and operation of autonomous vehicles.

- Liability in Accidents: Determining liability in the event of accidents involving autonomous vehicles.

6. AI Governance

Key Issues:

- Inclusive Policymaking: Involving diverse stakeholders, including technologists, ethicists, policymakers, and the public, in the creation of AI regulations.

- Adaptive Governance: Developing governance frameworks that can evolve with technological advancements and emerging challenges.

Challenges:

- Public Trust: Building public trust in AI systems and the regulatory frameworks governing them.

- Global Governance: Establishing global governance structures to address cross-border challenges and ensure cooperative oversight.

Glossary of AI Terms

A

1. Artificial Intelligence (AI): The simulation of human intelligence by machines, especially computer systems, performing tasks such as learning, reasoning, problem-solving, and understanding language.

2. Algorithm: A set of step-by-step instructions for solving a problem or performing a task.

3. Artificial General Intelligence (AGI): A type of AI that possesses the ability to understand, learn, and apply knowledge across a wide range of tasks, much like a human being.

B

4. Backpropagation: A training algorithm for neural networks, where the error is propagated backward through the network to update the weights.

5. Bias: A systematic error introduced into AI models due to inaccurate assumptions in the learning algorithm or training data.

C

6. Classification: A type of supervised learning where the goal is to predict the category or class of an input based on its features.

7. Clustering: An unsupervised learning technique that groups similar data points together based on their features.

8. Convolutional Neural Network (CNN): A deep learning model particularly effective for analyzing visual data, such as images and videos.

D

9. Data Mining: The process of discovering patterns and knowledge from large amounts of data.

10. Data Preprocessing: The process of cleaning and transforming raw data into a format suitable for analysis.

11. Deep Learning: A subset of machine learning involving neural networks with many layers (deep neural networks) that can learn complex patterns in data.

12. Decision Tree: A supervised learning algorithm that splits data into branches based on decision rules derived from the data's features.

E

13. Epoch: One complete pass through the entire training dataset.

14. Ensemble Learning: A machine learning technique that combines multiple models to improve performance and robustness.

F

15. Feature Extraction: The process of transforming raw data into numerical features that can be used for machine learning.

16. Feature Selection: The process of selecting a subset of relevant features for model construction.

G

17. Generative Adversarial Network (GAN): A type of neural network composed of two networks, a generator and a discriminator, that compete against each other to produce realistic synthetic data.

18. Gradient Descent: An optimization algorithm used to minimize the loss function in machine learning models by iteratively adjusting model parameters.

H

19. Hyperparameters: Parameters that govern the training process of a machine learning model and are set before training begins.

20. Hierarchical Clustering: A clustering technique that builds a hierarchy of clusters by progressively merging or splitting existing clusters.

I

21. Instance-Based Learning: A type of learning algorithm that compares new problem instances with instances seen in training, which have been stored in memory.

22. Interpretability: The extent to which a human can understand the decisions made by an AI system.

J

23. Jaccard Index: A statistic used for gauging the similarity and diversity of sample sets.

K

24. K-Means Clustering: A popular unsupervised learning algorithm used to partition data into k distinct clusters based on feature similarity.

25. Kernel: A function used in support vector machines (SVM) and other algorithms to transform data into a higher-dimensional space.

L

26. Label: The target variable that an algorithm is trying to predict.

27. Learning Rate: A hyperparameter that controls how much to change the model in response to the estimated error each time the model weights are updated.

28. Logistic Regression: A statistical model used for binary classification tasks.

M

29. Machine Learning (ML): A subset of AI that involves the development of algorithms that allow computers to learn from and make predictions based on data.

30. Model: A mathematical representation of a real-world process built using machine learning algorithms.

N

31. Natural Language Processing (NLP): A branch of AI focused on the interaction between computers and human language, enabling computers to understand, interpret, and generate human language.

32. Neural Network: A series of algorithms that attempt to recognize underlying relationships in a set of data through a process that mimics the way the human brain operates.

O

33. Overfitting: A modeling error in machine learning where a model learns the details and noise in the training data to an extent that it negatively impacts the model's performance on new data.

P

34. Precision: A metric used to evaluate the accuracy of a classification model, calculated as the number of true positives divided by the sum of true positives and false positives.

35. Principal Component Analysis (PCA): A dimensionality-reduction technique that transforms data into a set of orthogonal (uncorrelated) components ranked by their variance.

36. Predictive Analytics: The use of statistical techniques and machine learning algorithms to make predictions about future events based on historical data.

Q

37. Q-Learning: A reinforcement learning algorithm that seeks to find the best action to take given the current state by learning the value of state-action pairs.

R

38. Random Forest: An ensemble learning method that constructs multiple decision trees and merges them together to get a more accurate and stable prediction.

39. Recurrent Neural Network (RNN): A type of neural network designed for processing sequential data by maintaining a hidden state that captures information about previous inputs.

40. Reinforcement Learning (RL): A type of machine learning where an agent learns to make decisions by performing actions and receiving rewards or penalties.

41. Regression: A type of supervised learning task where the goal is to predict a continuous numeric value based on input features.

S

42. Semi-Supervised Learning: A type of learning that combines a small amount of labeled data with a large amount of unlabeled data during training.

43. Supervised Learning: A type of machine learning where the algorithm is trained on labeled data, meaning that each training example is paired with an output label.

44. Support Vector Machine (SVM): A supervised learning algorithm used for classification and regression tasks by finding the hyperplane that best separates the data into classes.

T

45. Tensor: A multi-dimensional array used in machine learning and deep learning to represent data.

46. Transfer Learning: A machine learning technique where a pre-trained model is reused on a new, related problem, allowing the model to leverage prior knowledge.

47. Training Data: The dataset used to train a machine learning model, containing input-output pairs.

U

48. Unsupervised Learning: A type of machine learning where the algorithm learns from unlabeled data by identifying patterns and structures in the input data.

V

49. Validation Data: A subset of the training data used to tune hyperparameters and evaluate the model's performance during training.

50. Vanishing Gradient: A problem in training deep neural networks where gradients become very small, making it difficult for the model to learn and update parameters.

W

51. Weights: Parameters in a neural network that are adjusted during training to minimize the error of the model.

X

52. XGBoost: A scalable and efficient gradient boosting framework used for supervised learning tasks, particularly for classification and regression.

Y

53. Yield: In the context of AI, it can refer to the output or results produced by a model or algorithm.

Z

54. Zero-Shot Learning: A method where the model can predict the correct label for new classes that were not seen during training, based on information transfer from known classes.

This glossary covers a broad range of key terms and concepts essential for understanding artificial intelligence and its various subfields.

www.ingramcontent.com/pod-product-compliance
Lightning Source LLC
Chambersburg PA
CBHW031237050326
40690CB00007B/844